# the monkey and the fish

**The Leadership Network Innovation Series**

*The Big Idea: Focus the Message, Multiply the Impact,* Dave Ferguson, Jon Ferguson, and Eric Bramlett

*Confessions of a Reformission Rev.: Hard Lessons from an Emerging Missional Church,* Mark Driscoll

*Deliberate Simplicity: How the Church Does More by Doing Less,* David Browning

*Leadership from the Inside Out: Examining the Inner Life of a Healthy Church Leader,* Kevin Harney

*The Multi-Site Church Revolution: Being One Church in Many Locations,* Geoff Surratt, Greg Ligon, and Warren Bird

*Sticky Church,* Larry Osborne

Other titles forthcoming

Will move you to seek opportunities to love God's people.

—Craig Groeschel, Pastor, LifeChurch.tv; author, *It*

Looks at the world and the church in a revolutionary way.

—Bob Buford, Founder, Leadership Network

Any who are willing to shape the future need to read this book.

—Neil Cole, author, *Organic Church*

A must-read for anyone who wonders about the relevance of church.

—Bill Clark, International Justice Mission

This book helps us see where the power to transform culture really lies.

—Richard Stearns, President, World Vision US

This book will stretch your thinking, and then it will stretch your faith.

—Gary Walter, President, The Evangelical Covenant Church

Provides insights that will initiate conversations and movements.

—Charles Lee, Lead Cultural Catalyst, New Hope

Speaks through simple stories whose implications are compelling.

—DJ Chuang, Executive Director, L2 Foundation

Leads the way in a movement that thinks globally and lives locally.

—Jim Orred, Youth with a Mission

Essential for how the church should be in the twenty-first century.

—Namjung Lee, Executive Pastor, Sarang Community Church, Seoul

This book will challenge you to be more daring for Christ.

—Daniel S. Kim, Pastor, Sa Rang Community Church, Anaheim

I commend this book to everyone who has a passion for relevancy and authenticity.

—Dave Anderson, Pastor, Bridgeway Community Church

Will challenge your view of our world and the role of the local church.

—Tony Morgan, Chief Strategic Officer, NewSpring Church

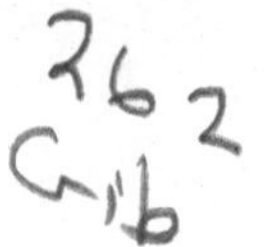

Full of honest reflections of a global thinker and innovator.

—Scott Hodge, Pastor, Orchard Valley Community Church

Beautifully honest insight into what the end-times church should be.

—Kong Hee, Pastor, City Harvest Church, Singapore

Poses uncomfortable questions and brings inspiring perspective.

—Mike Erre, Pastor, Rock Harbor Church

What you need to understand the emerging "third culture" church.

—Luis Bush, International Facilitator, Transform World Connections

Opens your eyes to a new way of being and doing church.

—Jaeson Ma, Lead Director, Campus Church Networks

A much-needed reminder that the church was meant to serve generously and graciously out in the world.

—James Choung, author, *True Story*

Calls us to a new way of being the church.

—Richard Peace, Fuller Theological Seminary

Could revolutionize ministry in the twenty-first century.

—Soong-Chan Rah, North Park Theological Seminary

Challenges us to new ways of imagining and living in the world.

—Stephen Hayner, Columbia Theological Seminary

A powerful and compelling invitation to ministry.

—Peter T. Cha, Trinity Evangelical Divinity School

# the monkey and the fish

## LIQUID LEADERSHIP FOR A THIRD-CULTURE CHURCH

dave gibbons

ZONDERVAN®

ZONDERVAN.com/
AUTHORTRACKER
*follow your favorite authors*

*The Monkey and the Fish*


This title is also available as a Zondervan ebook. Visit www.zondervan.com/ebooks.

This title is also available in a Zondervan audio edition. Visit www.zondervan.fm.

Requests for information should be addressed to:
Zondervan, *Grand Rapids, Michigan 49530*

---

**Library of Congress Cataloging-in-Publication Data**

Gibbons, Dave, 1962-
The monkey and the fish : liquid leadership for a third-culture church / Dave Gibbons.
p. cm.—(The leadership network innovation series)
Includes bibliographical references.
ISBN 978-0-310-27602-9 (softcover)
1. Church. 2. Christianity—21st century. 3. Globalization—Religious aspects—Christianity. I. Title.
BV600.3.G525 2009
262.001'7—dc22

2008033881

---



Published in association with Yates & Yates, www.yates2.com.

*Interior design by Ben Fetterley*

*Printed in the United States of America*

---

09 10 11 12 13 14 • 22 21 20 19 18 17 16 15 14 13 12 11 10 9 8 7 6 5 4

To Becca,
the love of my life,
who chooses third culture every day

To my children:
My prayer is that you know
the amazing favor of God on your lives.

To Newsong:
Thanks for your love. It frees me.

The evil that is in the world almost always comes of ignorance, and good intentions may do as much harm as malevolence if they lack understanding.

—Albert Camus

# Contents

# Foreword

It is sobering, vexing, dispiriting, and a lot of other lousy *-ing* things to realize how easy it is to lose perspective in life. But sometimes, if you're fortunate, you have an experience that hands a new perspective to you on a silver platter. And when you receive that gift, there's a good chance you'll not be the same.

I've received that gift many times.

As a journalist, I used to help cover space-shuttle launches at Kennedy Space Center. Seeing the space shuttle lurch off the pad at the space center from the news-media viewing area is like witnessing the eighth wonder of the world. It's a truly awesome display of human ingenuity and Newtonian physics.

And yet, after just a couple of launches, I'd lost that sense of awe. Worse yet, I was bugged. I had to set my alarm clock for 2:00 a.m. to get through NASA security on time. And then I had to wait forever in the wee hours of yet another humid Florida morning. And don't get me started on how irritating it was when they scrubbed a mission at the last possible second because of threatening weather or a potentially deadly technical problem.

Then I got invited to see a space-shuttle launch from a new perspective—strapped inside a Jolly Green Giant helicopter hovering at an altitude of eight thousand feet in "the Box." (That's what they call the restricted airspace and water surrounding the space center on launch days.) The Jolly Green was filled with pararescue jumpers ("PJs") and was standing by in case the shuttle had to abort or ditch in the seconds after liftoff. Inside the Jolly Green, I listened as the countdown hit zero and then watched *below* me as the shuttle roared off the pad, seemed to come straight toward us, and then gently arched away from the chopper and into space. Oh man. I've never, ever, looked at another space shuttle launch, on TV or on the web or anywhere else, quite the same. And really, ever since, I've looked at a lot of other things in life differently. That experience brought home the truth of an axiom that Alan Kay, a genius computer-science pioneer, observed—that a proper perspective is worth fifty IQ points.

I tell you this story because I believe who Dave Gibbons is and what he has to say has the same potential for impact.

Just as it's way too easy in life for individuals to lose perspective, the same thing can happen to institutions, organizations, and movements. The religious domain is no exception. In fact, it may be worse than most.

In this book Dave quotes somebody saying that Jesus is the trickiest part of the Christian faith to understand and the most difficult part for churches to keep alive. That gauntlet-dropping reality is what this book is all about. It's about the essence of Jesus. It's about renewing a proper perspective for this most extravagant, humble lover of humanity. It's especially game-altering for those who intend to do works in his name in the twenty-first century. And it's a manifesto for far-reaching change that couldn't be more timely.

Not long ago, I read that maybe churches have angels assigned to them. If this is true, it's good news. Because they're badly needed. Today, more than ever.

I've been around churches for much of my adult life, for both personal and professional reasons, and here are some things that are apparent:

You can be a church and lose your perspective on what activities are truly valuable.
You can be a church and have wrong motives, and they can be revealed only by a sort of divine X-ray that few seem willing to undergo.
You can be a church and be materially wealthy but spiritually famished and self-deceived.

This last item—deceit—looms especially large, because wrongdoing, whether in an individual or an organization, often starts with someone believing a lie, usually about themselves or someone else.

Today, too many churches:

Are opposed to the very things Jesus is for.
Avoid the very places Jesus would go.

Hold in contempt the very people Jesus would be most compassionate toward.

Dave Gibbons has something powerful, essential, and fresh to say on all of these subjects, and then some. Of all that I've read and heard, it's my conviction that Dave's voice is at the very top of those that deserve to be listened to and, more important, that we *need* to listen to.

When Dave looked out over his huge, "successful" church one Easter morning with all the stage lights and four-color programs and grinning parking attendants and all the other signs of his having "arrived," he suddenly wondered what he had wrought. And he had the guts and the humbleness to be honest and vulnerable about it, and to take daring counterintuitive actions—actions that ultimately led to the ideas introduced in this book.

When Dave jumped out of an airplane and his primary parachute failed to open and he was about twenty-three seconds from oblivion, he regarded it as an amazing adventure and a curious way to go out. (He also later professed gratitude for his backup chute.)

When Dave went to Skid Row in downtown Los Angeles and saw cat-sized rats skulking through the gutters and gangbangers flashing sets and teenaged "scramblers" on bikes warning dope dealers of approaching cops, he passed out water bottles and soup to homeless people, and gently placed his hands on some desperate guy's shoulders and whispered a prayer for him.

When Dave is in a meeting with his leaders—who are as ethnically, racially, demographically, and spiritually diverse a team as you'll ever find—it's very difficult discerning who the leader is. More often than not, Dave is listening. Closely.

Often, when Dave prays, he asks God to help him not to be a whiner, to have the ability to take abnormal joy in doing whatever small part he can to help people be relieved of at least a portion of their suffering. As best as I can tell, from having the privilege of being part of Dave's life these past few years, this prayer is being answered. And this, at least in the place where I grew up, speaks to the simple, undiluted charter of churches and of men and women of the cloth—relieving people of their suffering, restoring their sense of freedom, and increasing peace, grace, charity, mercy, and sacrifice, all the things that seem to be in short supply in this world.

Just as that ride in the Jolly Green chopper reset my perspective and restored my sense of awe, mystery, and clarity, the insights, lessons, and perspectives Dave articulates in this book can help you remember why you are doing what you are doing. Or even inspire you to dramatically shift your way of thinking. And while Dave is the least likely person to tell people how they should do what they do, it wouldn't be the worst thing if he did.

Since that is so unlikely, given what I know of my dear friend, it is no small thing that at least there is this book.

—J. J. Brazil

Pulitzer Prize–winning journalist

# Preface

A typhoon stranded a monkey on an island. In a protected place on the shore, while waiting for the raging waters to recede, he spotted a fish swimming against the current. It seemed to the monkey that the fish was struggling and needed assistance. Being of kind heart, the monkey resolved to help the fish.

A tree leaned precariously over the spot where the fish seemed to be struggling. At considerable risk to himself, the monkey moved far out on a limb, reached down, and snatched the fish from the waters. Scurrying back to the safety of his shelter, he carefully laid the fish on dry ground. For a few moments, the fish showed excitement but soon settled into a peaceful rest.

—An Eastern parable

Translation? The fish died!

Relevance to the twenty-first-century church?

Everything.

Our world is changing so rapidly, and more than ever, the church needs more than good intentions. We often enter a crisis with a great deal of enthusiasm, even compassion and heroism. But so often the result is tragic. Whether we're trying to reach a new generation or a foreign culture, we tend to proclaim. We often don't listen well. Too many times we resort to yesterday's answers and methods. But today, in a world driven by the forces of globalism, the crises and issues the church grapples with far exceed our sometimes simplistic and insular, if well-intended, approaches.

To effectively carry Jesus' gospel to various places around the globe today — more important, to *be* Jesus' gospel — listening is required. We need to be sensitive and lead with an eager learner's resolve. Those who follow Jesus embody fluidity, adaptation, and collaboration. It's what we call the third-culture way. Adaptable to changing circumstances. To challenging cultures. To complex crises and problems.

If there's one quality that matters most to the fate of the church in the twenty-first century, it's adaptability.

This is a colossal challenge for us. Historically, the church has been slow to embrace change and adapt to ethnic, cultural, and technological shifts. That's a problem because globalism — the intersecting of cultures that is happening today — is all about disruptive ethnic, economic, political, cultural, and technological shifts. Without adaptability, we're becoming increasingly out of touch with the global village taking shape around us.

Consider just some of the dynamics at work in our world today that the church must navigate and wade into effectively if we are to be successful in bringing, and being, the gospel to the global village.

Natural disasters
Drought
Global warming
Violence
Regime changes
Global power shifts
Poverty
Rising prices
Food shortages
War
Poor health care
Disease
Immigration
Terrorism
Postmodernism
Declining influence of the church

The problem is that formulas and one-size-fits-all programs so often do more harm than good. We need to learn to adapt, to be fluid—or liquid, a word I use a lot these days to assess my own abilities as a global citizen, follower of Jesus, and church leader.

To address the issues that mark today's world is not an easy task. This book may not solve any of these challenges, but it is a sober look at how we do church and measure making a difference.

To accomplish this, how about considering not only what we say and do but *how* we say and do it? Today, we cannot separate the what from the how, the message from the method. The issue is not just sharing our message but *becoming* the message. The form is just as important as the content. If the medium doesn't match the message, the message is incongruous. And since our message is Jesus' message—the extravagant love of God for a needy world—the stakes could not be higher.

We'll explore in this book the concept of being liquid, or being third culture. It's my heartfelt conviction that to the extent we can become third-culture churches and third-culture leaders, we'll not only adapt but thrive. We'll recognize that third culture is who God is. Jesus best embodied third culture when, as an "outsider" yet still the Son of God, he chose to fully live in the world that would eventually crucify him.

## A Third-Culture World

*Third culture* is a term used by sociologists and by foreign-service workers whose children are immersed in foreign cultures because of their parents' work. Sociologists observe that children in such circumstances feel compelled to come to terms with their indigenous culture but also must assimilate into the new culture their parents have plunged them into.

When third-culture kids become adults, they possess a heightened sensibility and intelligence about embracing and bridging cultural differences wherever they go. They're accomplished "culture-nauts," so to speak. Throughout their lives, they are able to relate to people of vastly different cultures far more easily than most people can. And because of their deeply ingrained convictions about the inherent richness and value of different cultures, worldviews, and perspectives, they seek to expose their own children to the diversity of the world's people and cultures. They celebrate culture. They treasure it. They respect it.

As we unpack the third-culture way, I think you'll see how it is at the core of the gospel and who we are called to become.

## My Story

This project is personal, and it's also about the love affair I have with the church. God stirred something in me to see where the church may be heading and what I was perpetuating. As I take a good look at the church, I do this realizing I am part of the problem.

I don't claim to be a theologian or a sociologist, but I sense from my travels and connections with many global leaders — including artists, business leaders, community-development specialists, executives of nongovernmental organizations, pastors, and spiritual leaders — that a major shift of historic proportions economically, politically, and spiritually has already occurred. The world and its rules have dramatically changed, but we are still having the modernism-postmodernism-emergent debate and discussing how to grow our suburban communities, often with the same result as when the monkey tried to save the fish.

It's not easy to admit this to ourselves, but the gap between our perception of the American church's influence and the reality is growing wider every hour. We live under the illusion that we are a Herculean force. But what many people around the world see is a version of Christianity created in our own cultural image, a Christianity with diminishing power and influence and filled with a lot of pride, self-centeredness, and wrongheaded metrics. Being part of the Western cultural machine, our American churches tend to gravitate toward the gods of pragmatism, materialism, and consumerism. And today, people around the world can't see anything supernatural about that. The global village is longing for something deeper. Sadly, fewer find it in a Western way of doing church.

I too believe that. There's something much better out there.

What if there were a second renaissance of the church? What if the church were at the forefront of innovations in the arts, business, justice, compassion, and advocacy? What if the church became known for being great partners rather than for insisting on our own movements and branding? What if there were a stirring of regional and national Spirit-led movements in which millions of people were being transformed through Jesus—from among the lowest social castes of India, to the hill tribes of Thailand, to the underground movements of China, to the young artists in Mexico City, to the pubs of London, and to the suburbs and urban centers of America?

I'm hoping this book will help us to take a fresh look at what we have built and be open to considering a new yet old way, the way of third culture.

## One Liquid Leader

Not long ago, a story in the news enchanted people around the world.

Every night, Julio Diaz, a thirty-one-year-old social worker, ended his hour-long subway commute to the Bronx one stop early so he could eat at his favorite diner.

But one night, when Diaz stepped off the No. 6 train and into the deserted station, something unexpected happened. He was headed toward the stairs when a teenager suddenly appeared and whipped out a knife.

When the assailant demanded Julio's money, he calmly handed him his wallet.

Nothing so unusual about that.

But as the young robber turned away, Diaz called out to him.

"Hey, wait a minute," Diaz said. "You forgot something. If you're going to be robbing people for the rest of the night, you might as well take my coat to keep you warm."

The boy was dumbfounded. He looked at Diaz with a what-in-the-world look and asked, "Why are you doing this?"

Diaz told him, "If you're willing to risk your freedom for a few dollars, then I guess you must really need the money."

Diaz told the boy that he was on his way to get dinner and said that if the boy was hungry, he could join him.

So they went to the diner and plopped down in a booth together, and when several employees came by to greet Diaz, one of their regular customers, he kindly introduced the boy to them.

Stunned by the evening's turn of events, the robber asked Diaz how it was that he knew everyone there and remarked on how he was nice to everyone, "Even the dishwasher."

Diaz asked him if he hadn't also been taught to be kind to everyone. The boy told him he had, but he didn't think people acted that way in the real world.

The conversation turned a bit more serious when Diaz asked him what he wanted out of life.

The boy didn't express much of an answer.

When the tab came, Diaz told the teen he was going to have to pay the bill, since he had taken his wallet, unless he wanted to give it back, in which case, Diaz said, he'd be happy to pay the whole thing, his treat.

According to Diaz, the teen "didn't even think about it" and handed over the wallet. Besides treating him to dinner, Diaz gave him twenty dollars, just something to help him out.

In return, Diaz asked for his knife, and the boy, who'd threatened Diaz with that same knife not long before, quickly surrendered it.

Afterward, Diaz said that treating people right, regardless of how they treat you, is the simplest and most promising prescription he knows to bring people hope and to make the world a better place.

Why did National Public Radio air another story of a mugging in America? Because Julio's response was third culture. It was an embrace of pain and an extension of generosity—learning, loving, and serving all wrapped in one amazing young man.

Before reading on, pause and take a moment to experience third culture. Check out http://3culture.tv.

# Acknowledgments

This book is about becoming water, learning to adapt and become all things to all people. It's about being like Jesus, who is the living water. Many men and women have guided and influenced me in learning how to become fluid yet true in an ever-changing culture. I am deeply indebted to each of the following:

Jeff Brazil: The best surprise in doing this book was the birth of an engaging friendship with you. Thank you for your patience and care in helping me write this book.

Jim Gustafson: You are the Yoda of third culture. You live third culture and have embodied it since before I was born. Thank you for inspiring me and encouraging me to come to see Thailand, your life, and your work. I'll never be the same again.

Adam Edgerly: You're one of the brilliant profs of third culture. Thanks for the insights and interaction about this beloved subject of ours.

The Third-Culture Pioneers: Dave and Jill Brubaker, Cue Jean-Marie, Susie Lee, Bryan Belden, Benny and Janice

Yu, Brian Kim, Daniel and Sadie Kim, Mehta and Lydia Kriengparinyakij, Peter and Patricia DeWitt, Lon and Aey, Yo Warong, Jamie and Brenda Strombeck, Abe and Annette Park, Steven Peters, Jimmy and Jessica Lee.

Chong Randolph, my sister, who believed that even though some of our childhood was rough, God would give us the privilege of making a difference on this earth. Thanks for sacrificing for me!

The community of churches that demonstrated an amazing amount of patience and love for me and my family, gave me a love for the church, and allowed me space to work through these concepts: Newsong and our staff (the whole alliance of communities), Bethel, Onnuri, Tri-City, Evangelical Covenant, Northwest Bible Church, and Korean Presbyterian Church of Dallas (now Binnerri Church).

Some childhood friends of mine who prayed for me and stirred a flame in me for the church to impact the world, a flame that burns to this day. Thanks Mike, Kevin, Larry, Dave, and Matthew.

Mentors who, whether they know it or not, gave me a love for third culture and the church: Dr. Cho and Dr. Chung from Baltimore Bethel Church; Dr. Youn and the Nehemiah team; Dr. David Sang Bok Kim; Dr. Young Jo Hah (probably one of the greatest visionaries on the planet); Howard Hendricks; Jim Rose; Bill Lawrence; Darrell Bock; Leighton Ford; Bob Buford; Max DePree; Jim Orred; Susie Lee and her late husband, Chong Lee, who believed in me and the third-culture movement from day one and backed it with sacrificial support; Dr. Richard Peace; Bill Hybels; Rick Warren; Ray Johnston; Erwin McManus; Bob Roberts; Gordon MacDonald; Luis Bush; Dr. Michael Stitzinger; Bob Shank and Denny Bellesi, who gave me the opportunity I needed to start Newsong; Dr. Charles Smith; Gary Walters; Ken Fong; Dave Olson; Richard Stearns and the board of World Vision US; the late Helen Stroup, who prayed all through college that God would send more pain into my life (can you believe that?!); my mother and father, Son Chae Gibbons and Gary W. Gibbons; Dave Bunt, who saw something in me when I was a prodigal (Dave, thanks for not listening to the crowd who told you to not bother with me); and Henri Nouwen, who changed my life.

My friends who, from different domains, are artfully being water to the world: Mike Wang, Paul Kim, Darryl Brumfield, Henry Ho, Bill Rhee, Bill Hwang, Peter Cha, Bronnie Lee, Lincoln and Susan Snyder, Ho and Mehee Kim, Rich and Suzan Paek, Paul and Annie Kim, John Park, Brenda Salter McNeil, John and Dawn Kennedy, Willie Kim, Ted Tanouye, Dave Chae, Doug Finkbeinner, Peter Cha, Bryan Loritts, Alex Gee, and Mike Foster.

And Peter Nguyen, my assistant: You rock! Thanks for flowing with me all these years.

current 1

# Liquid

> The desire for safety stands against every noble human endeavor.
>
> —Tacitus, Roman philosopher

> I'm for truth, no matter who tells it. I'm for justice, no matter who it is for or against. I'm a human being, first and foremost, and as such I'm for whoever and whatever benefits humanity as a whole.
>
> —Malcolm X

The rebellious, disrespectful, disillusioned, and demanding Prodigal Son is the focus of one of the most glorious moments in the Gospels. Yet the real highlight of that passage in Luke 15 is the radically gracious, generous, and forgiving father.

I love that story because it's Eastern in its cultural tone. Normally, an Eastern father would never run toward his son. The typical Eastern son, with head bowed, would be quick to demonstrate obeisance to his father. However, this father is different. This father runs and, in what is considered by many to be the most intimate portrait of love in the Bible, kisses his son over and over again. Most versions of the Bible don't translate these repeated kisses. The kisses of the father. Kisses that entwine forgiveness, celebration, and blessing.

The world longs for such kisses from the Father.

No one should be in a better position to fulfill this longing than the church. Who can give a better kiss than the church? A kiss without strings attached. A supernatural kiss that can set captives free. A kiss that inspires prodigals to remember real love and to come back home.

I sometimes think how sweet it would be if that were the reaction of every person, every family, every neighbor, every community, even every country, whenever they come into contact with those of us who follow Jesus, who make up the church.

I think it could happen.

I believe that today God is calling us in the church to become a different kind of movement, known for our kisses of compassion rather than our condemnations.

I'm not sure there's ever been a better opportunity for those of us in the church to do so. A historic coming together of many unusual forces are shaping today's global village. Our world is marked by unprecedented degrees of multiculturalism, social advocacy, international collaboration and interdependence, and technology-driven outbreaks of freedom, unity, and community. They provide an intersection, a *kairos* moment, in which the church can shine.

From its first moments, the church has held the promise of being an expression of God's presence on this earth. No other entity has greater potential to bring about real and sustainable change for good, whether we're talking about individual lives or the world at large.

But something's wrong. In North America, there has been a steady decline in church attendance, church giving, and church participation, a pattern we've already seen unfold in Europe, once the seat of Christianity's global expansion. These are signs of a much larger problem: the erosion of the significance of the church in the public square and in people's personal lives. In the spring of 2006, a national poll in America indicated that only 17 percent of Americans said going to church is essential for a life of faith.

### Altered States

Around the world, things are changing fast these days, and in ways that seemed unthinkable only a few years ago. Just ask any of the people who attended a recent World Economic Forum in Davos, Switzerland. This annual gathering draws some of the most influential people in the world, including people from all fields—religion, politics, media, business, you name it. There was plenty of talk about novel business strategies and potential political partnerships. But people who are students of culture couldn't help but notice that new topics and questions are looming large in the most important conversations taking place today. There are conversations about how China is upending the world economy and culture, and about how China is eclipsing the United States in so many ways. There are conversations about how grassroots social change around the globe—which is being fueled by the internet's vast potential for helping people leap barriers of time, distance, and culture—is far outstripping institutional approaches to crises and problem-solving, whether the institution is political or religious or otherwise.

There are conversations about how the world demands that business not only be good for profits but also be good for the planet and good for people. In business, it used to be that one bottom line—profit—separated the good from the bad. Now there are at least two bottom lines to attend to: profit and cause. This new reality, this new way of doing things, has huge ramifications for the thinking, methods, and game plans of for-profit organizations and business entities of all kinds. Many in the corporate and nonprofit domains are pretty sleep-deprived these days trying to figure out this new world we live in and what it means to be cause-oriented and socially conscious with their gains. This is in large part because they recognize the profitability of cause marketing.

What does all of this have to do with those of us in the church? Well, just as the spheres of commerce and government are being fundamentally reshaped by globalism, so is the domain of the church. Again, it's not new but a wake-up call to return to our roots, our calling as lovers of the marginalized.

*Globalism* applies to the many colossal shifts occurring in the world today because of an intense interdependence that countries, cultures, and people are experiencing with one another. The world is shrinking. By the day, it seems. Distances that once took months to cover now take hours. People and cultures unknown to us, let alone ever personally encountered by us, are an integral part of the fabric of our lives. For example, experts have said that if you take out the undocumented worker in places like California, that will wreak havoc on our economy. People in politics and business, in education and the arts, people throughout all of our institutions, are finding it difficult to keep up with the way the world is changing, to understand what's happening and why, and to adapt.

I love the church. But the church historically has proven slow to embrace necessary change and to adapt to ethnic, sociological, and cultural shifts. It's like we know we're unhealthy but we don't want to go to the doctor to take care of the problem. And I don't think it has been any different with globalism. I'm concerned that with globalism, the nature and scope of the changes taking place in the world are so sweeping and the pace of change so unrelenting that we're becoming increasingly out of touch with the reality of our sickness.

At the risk of oversimplifying things, globalism truly is what historians call a disruptive force, because it's making for a very different, new world: culturally, economically, socially, technologically, commercially, and politically.

There are difficult, troubling aspects to this reshaping, but also wonderful possibilities. For instance, the collective threats posed worldwide by terrorism, pandemics, rogue military leaders, political and social corruption, environmental complexities, and racism are frightening and daunting. But I also see an unprecedented potential for creative international and cross-cultural collaboration because we are living in a cause-driven culture. It's now hip to be advocates of justice and compassion. In fact, people everywhere are hungering for authentic spiritual conversations and opportunities to change the world. I look at the spiritual movements taking place in China, India, and Southeast Asia and they leave me breathless. Around the planet, there is an openness not only to doing good but to experiencing Jesus and his teachings, and it's growing exponentially.

The church has an amazing opportunity to become what God is hoping we will become. It'll take the resculpting of our organizations and corporate culture, the incubation of new art forms, new languages and expressions, new symbols, flexible ways of being organized and led, and even a fuller explanation of what we know as the gospel. (See how one MIT graduate is reimagining the gospel. Search on these words: *James Choung Story* at http://youtube.com. The type of work James is doing is exactly the work that each generation must do.) We need creative forms, methods, and practices for sharing the truth we love and believe in that will work in the new world and with a new generation. We need fresh counterintuitive ways of leading—in practice and in philosophy.

As I travel around the world and talk to people, I hear many of us in the church expressing similar concerns and longings. We're looking for something that fits what we know to be intrinsically true. We're hungry for it. We sense the urgency of it.

Not one of us in the church has *the* answer, but I am fortunate enough to be surrounded by a group of young, multigenerational, multiethnic leaders and servants who have stumbled onto something that seems to have a lot of promise in the new world we all find ourselves in. It's something we call third culture. And these leaders that I'm discovering in cities all over the world, including America, are what we call third-culture leaders. It's something we in the group of churches we've launched feel pretty strongly about. We've seen an application of third-culture concepts ignite some beautiful things as we've put them into practice around the world.

A third-culture church and a third-culture leader look at our global milieu and the church's role in that milieu in a revolutionary way.

## The Third-Culture Mandate

When we understand the powerful force of globalism—possibly the single most significant macro influence impacting the world today—we'll understand how third-culture churches and third-culture leaders can help sustain and revitalize the church.

When I use the term *third-culture church*, I'm referring to a beautiful yet sobering reality: whether we're in Manhattan or Beijing or Sao Paulo, our credibility and the veracity of our initiatives will be measured by our third-culture lifestyles—hence the need to understand the third-culture mandate in light of the purposes of the church prioritized by Jesus himself when he was queried about the greatest commandment.

Third culture illuminates the dramatic changes in the world today as well as the insular and exclusive nature of the church. Yet by pursuing what a third-culture church and its leaders might look like in principle and practice, we'll be able to fulfill what Christ envisioned his church to be about.

In what some people have called the First Great Commission, God told Abraham that he and his offspring would be a "blessing to *all* the nations." That, I believe, is our charter, our call, for our churches to be a true blessing to all the nations. And the nations have never been more ready and eager for the church to offer the supernatural kiss of blessing it can offer.

I hope to be able to show you why and how the world is craving a third-culture spirit from the church and third-culture leaders within the church. We'll also discover together that third-culture thinking and practices can help the church not only have an impact globally but also reexamine how we do church and develop leaders to connect with our twenty-first-century global village—a place that has gone through a hundred years of change in just the past decade.

## Defining Third Culture

A working definition of third culture emerges from Genesis 12 and from the second greatest commandment: *Third culture is the mindset and will to love, learn, and serve in any culture, even in the midst of pain and discomfort.* From Genesis to Revelation you can track God's relentless pursuit of blessing humanity in the midst of man's rebellion. As you examine Genesis 1–12 again, you'll discover that the first mention of the Great Commission isn't in the book of Matthew but right here in Genesis 12, where God says that we are "blessed to be a blessing to the nations." This blessing is revealed in the conclusion of the Bible in Revelation 5:9–14, where all the nations are gathered singing a new song.

The hard work of this definition is the last phrase—"even in the midst of pain and discomfort." It is contrary to our nature and culture to embrace pain, but it is the catalyst for helping people to see God. As this book unfolds, you'll discover that third culture is not just a trend or a new thing but the heart of God. In fact, God is third culture.

Third culture is not only about geography or skin color or language. For third-culture people, home is wherever Jesus is. Third culture is the bearing of pain to love those who are not like you. Third culture affirms one's ethnic identity. One's ethnicity is not ignored but celebrated! Third culture doesn't dull the color of one's culture. Third culture actually enhances a culture's uniqueness while at the same time celebrating the synergy of its fusion with other cultures. Third culture artfully flows in and out of multiple cultures like water.

Here's another way of looking at it. First culture is the dominant homogeneous culture you live in. First culture tends to be more preservation-oriented, but that doesn't mean people don't take great risks. (For example, Asian immigrants often give up their status and wealth in their mother countries for the promise of better opportunities for their children in another country.) Second culture is the culture of those who aren't quite comfortable with the first culture and often react to the first culture's ways, maybe even rejecting their parents' home culture. Third culture is being able to live in both first and second culture and even adopt an entirely different culture. Third culture is about adaptation, the both/and, not the either/or, mindset. It doesn't eradicate color or lines but embraces and affirms who we are, regardless of differences in ethnicity, culture, or mindset. Third culture is the gift of being more cognizant of and more comfortable with the painful fusion and friction inherent in cultural intersections.

Others have also done some profound thinking about diversity, multiculturalism, multiethnicity, multigenerationalism, and other important topics that need attention. The challenge, I think, is that the solutions offered are often at best cosmetic, such as admonitions to hire more people of color, do pulpit exchanges, or include more music styles on Sunday mornings. Such common cultural initiatives often fall short of true racial reconciliation and lack depth.

## Scars: Generating Breakthroughs

Stephen "Cue" Jean-Marie is a rapper with a penchant for quoting Malcolm X. He grew up in the slums of the West Indies. Not long ago, he ended up at Newsong Church's campus in Irvine, California, a place where some would never expect a person like Cue to show up, let alone take a leadership role. But he did show up. And not long after, he took on an extraordinary challenge. Members of the congregation and leaders at Newsong in Irvine wanted him to find the most marginalized community in Los Angeles, the kind of place that some people at Newsong would be uncomfortable to be in. We asked him to find a way for Newsong to make a difference in such a place.

This was no easy task—on so many levels.

First, there's Cue himself. His stature is intimidating. He's a bodybuilder! He's not a seminary-trained church leader. He was weaned on the streets, really. He has scars on his muscular forearms from being branded with hot spoons in his childhood, somebody's sad idea of discipline. He's an unlikely pastor.

Then there's the people. To put it mildly, people in urban Los Angeles and suburban Orange County can be somewhat uncomfortable with one another. Los Angeles is a sprawling ethnically diverse county of ten million people, some of whom live in some of the most impoverished, crime-ridden places in America. Orange County is akin to what you see on suburban prime-time reality shows (well, sort of), a place overflowing with wealth, excessive tastes, corporate executives, racial homogeneity, and a pretty manic pursuit of a lifestyle filled with ease and good fortune. When someone leaves one of these counties and crosses the border of the other, they can be met with an unspoken "good riddance."

And then there's the challenge. How would Cue find a place in Los Angeles that would trust the intentions and methods of an Orange County megachurch? And would the Crenshaw community accept a legit urbanite and a man of the streets who had joined forces with a suburban megachurch? Even if Cue found such a place, what could a congregation in suburban Orange County possibly do that would be meaningful and valuable in a city radically different from Irvine? How could Cue persuade people in Orange County to embrace whatever cause and constituency he discovered?

These barriers were just the beginning. But it's the number and nature of the barriers, and the degree of unlikelihood involved in this mission, that make Cue's effort so remarkable. Looking back at it now, it's something that God himself had to be part of for it to work.

Cue met the challenge by forming a partnership with what is arguably the most troubled school in Los Angeles, a community where the majority of the children come from single-parent homes, where in one recent week seven students were shot to death in suspected gang activity, where the high school recently lost its accreditation.

Besides being committed to helping the high school regain its accreditation, the initiative Cue leads today employs sports, health education, the arts, wellness disciplines, mentoring, and whatever else might help to lift some of the burdens of the young people he deals with, and maybe even alter the trajectory of their lives.

Every day, Cue peers into the eyes of kids who are suffering in the same way he once did. And they see him as someone who doesn't need an explanation, who understands, who knows. The neighborhoods he spends his days in are busting at the seams with fatherless boys ill-equipped to do more than plant the seeds of another fatherless generation and with emotionally crippled girls settling for the crumbs of what passes for affection. Others drive through and around this area, but against some tall odds, Cue and his brothers and sisters in the Newsong community are living out what Mother Teresa gently instructed all of us to do: "If you cannot feed a hundred children, well then, feed one."

Cue and some of his crew of former gang members are sought-after partners by the schools in Crenshaw. Young people are clamoring to be part of their club. Lives are being changed. Now Cue has launched another ministry in Los Angeles called the Row, working with one of the most neglected people groups in Los Angeles: the homeless. Despite the noise of helicopters flying overhead and police cars whizzing by with their sirens going, they do church every Friday night on an open street corner with drug addicts and alcoholics and, believe it or not, suburbanites from Orange County.

How did Cue pull this off? Was it simply the result of his innate leadership skills? Certainly that's part of the explanation. But more intriguing is how Cue even ended up in the Newsong community. What attracted him to a community of ethnicities and cultures that are different from his? And how is it that he, not exactly prototypical leadership material for an American megachurch, came to be loved and empowered by Newsong to take on such a dangerous and meaningful mission?

The answer to all these questions finds its home in Cue's pain. Cue epitomizes a new breed of leader, a leader who leads from what I call the pain principle. This is one of several attributes that mark a third-culture leader and a third-culture church. The pain principle grows out of two axioms: (1) For leaders, pain in life has a way of deconstructing us to our most genuine, humble, authentic selves. It's part of the leader's job description. (2) For most people, regardless of culture, it's easier to connect with a leader's pain and shortcomings and mistakes than her successes and triumphs.

One of the things I'm learning as I encounter people around the world today is that leaders who understand the pain principle are the kind of leaders the world is thirsting for. What's intriguing to me is that this is the kind of leader the church was full of in its earliest days. Paul, Rahab, Ruth, Moses, Joseph, and Jesus himself were all such leaders. The apostle Paul, one of the greatest followers of Jesus, had a story similar to Cue's. He said, "From now on, don't let anyone trouble me with these things. For I bear on my body the scars that show I belong to Jesus" (Gal. 6:17 NLT). Paul is basically saying, "I have the right to speak to you because of these scars, evidence of Christ in me."

## Fuel the Fringe, Honor the Past

The church is called to be a third-culture community. Third culture is about the two purposes of life for every Christ-follower: loving God and loving your neighbor.

Without question, there are a lot of effective strategies and fruitful ideas being used in the church and in ministry today. Third culture is not simply a strategy but the way we are to live. One may not be naturally third culture, but we are called to move toward this vision. It seems that more than ever the world is open to such leadership. I say this simply because we have experienced it in communities where we seriously pursued a third-culture lifestyle in diverse cultural contexts spanning several continents and saw how people gravitate toward this adaptive, liquid-type leader. Even the next US president is third culture. As of this writing, we don't know whether the next president will be Obama or

McCain, but both have third-culture characteristics from their past and present.

### Any Church, Any Size, Anywhere

When my brother and I were teenagers, we were bottomless pits. We could consume massive quantities of food. My poor mom. She found really only one place she could take us that would satisfy us: the Royal Fork, an all-you-can-eat buffet where we ate for three to four hours at a sitting.

I can still picture the luscious spread. For my brother and me, nothing was more glorious than checking out every nook and cranny of that steamy buffet table and then consuming everything in sight. Buffets were our little heaven on earth. Nothing brings people together like good food!

That whole scene reminds me of a story in Luke 14 about another banquet that is jam-packed with prophetic power for us in the new millennium.

Jesus tells the story of a great feast being prepared in the kingdom of God. The host of the banquet has worked feverishly and is enthusiastic about this feast. So he dispatches a servant to visit all of the people who were invited to the banquet to make sure they are coming. One by one, however, they all tell the servant they aren't going to be able to attend. They're busy attending to transactions and urgent matters. They appreciate the invitation but have to take a rain check.

In response, the deeply disappointed host deploys his servant to go throughout the city to invite everyone he sees to the banquet—the homeless, the crippled, the lame, the poor, anyone he encounters. The servant lobs invitations to all comers, and before long, it's clear the banquet tables are going to be filled after all with all manner of grateful, joyful people, people who are not too busy. Jesus quietly closes with the haunting admonition that not one of the people who were originally invited will taste the greatest buffet of all time.

Like all of Jesus' parables, there's plenty of mystery in this story for us to burrow into. What did he mean by this sad, jarring story? Well, to me, there's a message for us in the church today.

As I travel to different nations, I see God's beautiful sculpting hand creatively at work, as unmistakable as it is unobtrusive. Spectacular spiritual shifts are occurring. But I wonder if the church is sometimes too busy, too distracted, too inwardly focused to sense all that's happening, all that could be, all that will be—with us or without us. Is it possible that we are so consumed with managing churches and ministries and organizations that we're missing out on an international spiritual banquet like we've never seen before? Is it possible that the reality of the new world we're living in gives the church an opportunity we've never had before, a chance for the church to be what we've always dreamed it could be?

I believe the church is the embodiment of Jesus on this earth. Think about that. That means that there is no organization with greater potential to have an impact or to be a more potent force for good than a third-culture church that is unleashed. What other organization has that kind of reason for being?

This all might sound pie-in-the-sky. That's fine. But the God we serve and love has the widest idealistic streak of any of us. A baton is being passed today—in the world and in the church—and any church of any size in any place can accept that baton and run with it. God is raising up in our churches—and outside our churches, frankly—a new generation of prophets with voices and liquid leadership skills tailor-made for our times. And I hope that none of us misses it.

In writing this book, my hope is that we will sacrificially foster and prioritize next-generation thinking, next-generation methods, and next-generation leaders in the church so that the global movement Jesus began will be known first and foremost for sharing love without strings, healing, extravagant radical compassion, and radical reconciliation with the world so lovingly breathed into existence by our creator.

## Shaping What Could Be

In addition to prayer and reflection on the state of the world these days, I've drawn from intentional experiential forays into nonprofit and for-profit work to better understand third-culture language and concepts, including my twenty years as a lead pastor developing churches both big and small, homogeneous and multicultural; from learning from some of the incredible leaders of churches and Christian movements and organizations in North America, the Far East, the United Kingdom, and India; from adventures as a board member with World Vision and as founder of Xealot, a nonprofit organization that seeks to help people living in marginalized communities; from involvement with two global cause-oriented for-profit ventures, one a financial trading house in California and the other a music label in Los Angeles; and from serving as a consultant and counselor for young artists, business leaders, and musicians on several continents.

In my journeys, what's becoming clear to me is that the more adaptive we are to the Holy Spirit and to diverse people groups and settings, the more we reflect who Jesus is and impact this new flat world.

Author Thomas Friedman has become a bit of a prophetic voice in this regard in the area of culture, politics, and business. In his seminal book, *The World Is Flat*, he describes some of the forces at work that are creating the groundwork and necessity for a third-culture movement in the church: "Two aspects of culture have struck me as particularly relevant in the flat world. One is how outward your culture is: To what degree is it open to foreign influences and ideas? How well does it 'glocalize' (a term that combines the necessity of both local and global initiatives—it's not a choice)? The other, more intangible, is how inward your culture is."[1] In other words, organizations with cultures that intentionally or unintentionally maintain an inward focus—a culture of exclusivity and a leeriness of and even suspicion toward differences and change—are in real trouble in this twenty-first-century global village of ours. Conversely, the more an organization's culture naturally glocalizes—the more easily our local cultures can absorb and embrace foreign ideas and best practices and meld those with the best of our traditions and values—the greater the boon we will enjoy in the new world.

This new reality is the sweet spot of third culture.

Now, for all of the challenges before us, there's great news for those of us who are privileged enough to be agents of the good news of God's love. The urgent changes globalism is prompting the church to make, I believe, are what God himself would prescribe for us. I say this simply because of what I see in Scripture that reveals God's impassioned, undeniable desire for the church's role in the world. What begins in Genesis with a call for God's people to be a blessing to all nations ends climactically in Revelation 7, where "all nations and tribes, all races and languages" are gathered together worshiping God. No matter how many times I read that passage, I never cease to feel lifted and emboldened to do whatever I can to help make that scene come to pass.

I don't think we can imagine the degree of the exquisite beauty that that moment described in Revelation will bring. But we get to see a sliver of it when, on rare moments in world events, we witness people laying aside their differences and coming together for good. There's something about that kind of unity and reconciliation that moves us beyond words. Likewise, that portrait in Revelation—a depiction of the climactic reconciliation of God and the chief object of his love, humankind—lies at the core of the message, methodology, and motivation of third culture.

If Friedman's bestselling *The World Is Flat* is an inspiring call to a different mindset about the world for business, culture, and government, then I think there's an urgent call for the church to do likewise.

We have much to learn from the world. A recent example is the opening ceremony of the 2008 Olympics in Beijing. It left many people in the world speechless. The scale and pageantry of the event were unprecedented. But beyond the amazing artistry of the event, one could feel that this was a coming out party for China and for Asia. Once known primarily for its illegal copying of products, Asia is increasingly known for its creativity. David Brooks, *New York Times* op-ed columnist, had an insightful take on this ceremony. He writes, "The world can be divided many ways—rich and poor, democratic and authoritarian—but one of the most striking is the divide between the societies with an individualistic mentality and the ones with a collectivist mentality."[2] Brooks then refers to a study by professor of psychology Richard Nesbitt in which Americans and Asians were shown individual pictures of a chicken, a cow, and hay. When they were asked which of the pictures go together, Americans typically picked the two animals. Asians typically picked the cow and the hay, since cows eat hay. Americans tend to see categories, whereas Asians are more likely to see relationships. That's why doing business in Asia is about more than signing a contract; it's about relationships of trust.

Often the Western world focuses on privacy and individual rights, whereas the Asian world focuses more on collective harmony, collective society. Brooks writes, "People in [individualistic] societies tend to overvalue their own skills and overestimate their own importance to any group effort. People in collective societies tend to value harmony and duty. They tend to underestimate their own skills and are more self-effacing when describing their contributions to group efforts." In a world in which the healthiest people tend to be in community and those prone to depression and suicide tend to be disconnected, we have much to learn from our "neighbors." The real value of our growing relationship with nations such as China will probably be more relational and community oriented than economic. We'll learn to look beyond categories and see relationships. That's third culture.

current 2

# Wardrobe

> In religion and politics, people's beliefs and convictions are in almost every case gotten at second hand, and without examination.
>
> —Mark Twain

> In conflict, straightforward actions generally lead to engagement, surprising actions generally lead to victory.... In war, numbers alone confer no advantage.
>
> —Sun Tzu, *The Art of War*

Remember when you were little, and when your dad or mom wasn't home, sometimes you tried on their clothes? You put on Dad's clothes and they didn't quite fit, but it felt cool to wear his big suit jacket and pretend you were the man. His masculine scent was on the coat, and you went ahead and tried on his pants too. They didn't fit at all, but you felt nearer to adulthood. But as you got older, you never wore your dad's Costco stuff because Urban Outfitters clothing was much hipper. You wouldn't think of it because your threads reflect you.

The more I think about it, the more I wonder, Is this what has happened to the church? As we've grown, have we donned clothes that really don't fit? I'll be honest, I think that's what happened to me.

I entered the ministry hoping to make a difference in the world. I still remember as a high school student praying with a small group of like-minded zealous students that God would use us to change the world. Little did I know how that prayer would change my life's course. A few years later, my mom died in a traffic accident when she was struck by a drunk driver. She died instantly. I still remember sitting dazed in her funeral service when I felt God saying, "I want you to give your life to me, to give yourself completely to me." For me, that meant I had to exchange my pursuit of money, which I have to admit was my focus, for the pursuit of God.

As a bright-eyed, idealistic young pastor-in-training, you learn quickly that churches have stealth bottom lines too. I think we are preoccupied with big.

While profit numbers might not be the goal of churches, congregational numbers sure are. Usually one of the first questions you're asked is, "So how big is your church?"

## Fishtank

If you show an American and an Asian a tank filled with several fish, what do you think they'll see? A study found that the American focused on the biggest fish's activity, while the Asian focused on the context, not just the fish.[3] For many of us, it's all about the big fish.

I went to church conferences as an impressionable young pastor and listened closely to the pastors of the largest growing churches in the Western world. I learned from these leading churches that what we need to do in pastoring a church is perform demographic research. Only then can we create a target person and a target group to focus on reaching. There were interesting names given to these targets, names like Unchurched Harry and Unchurched Mary and Saddleback Sam. Rick Warren and Bill Hybels warned us not imitate them, but when you're young and feel the need to make it happen, you tend to plug and play rather than innovate and pray.

So I did this. I kept at it. And it worked. Our church grew. Fast. In fact, we became one of the One Hundred Fastest Growing Churches in America. Looking back, that list seems pretty silly to me now. But at the time, it was kind of like a dream. Even though a "godly" pastor probably wouldn't say it, it's one of the dreams you'd like to achieve—for your church to become one of the biggest, and then for your church to keep getting bigger, because you believe that with bigness comes influence, and with influence you make a greater impact—for the kingdom of God, of course! Look at who speaks at the conferences. How many times have you seen a pastor of twenty-five people speak at the main plenary session at a pastor's conference?

It's not just about being big, of course. Any pastor would say the goal is to see lives transformed. But the fact is, we're taught that numbers reflect a healthy church. Again, numbers aren't the only thing. But we're told that if your church is truly healthy, you're going to reproduce and grow. It's a visible bottom line that people interpret to mean that something good is happening at your church.

## Easter Epiphany

In about year ten of our church's existence, after going through a fundraising campaign and a building expansion, I slowly started becoming cynical. I grew increasingly reticent. I found myself moving faster and faster. I felt like I had built an impressive machine that was running on high-octane fuel, but something didn't seem right. I couldn't put my finger on it at first. We drew the crowds. Our huge productions would rival some MTV specials, but I started becoming more and more disillusioned.

I'll never forget the Easter we rented the Anaheim Convention Center in Southern California to do our weekend services. It was a surreal moment. We had thousands of people. Just masses of volunteers out there. Balloons. Krispy Kreme donuts galore. We were in the shadow of the world-famous Magic Kingdom. Literally. The Anaheim Convention Center is right across the street from Disneyland Theme Park.

We had all these parking lot attendants trying to avoid getting hit. Crews of sound engineers. Cameras everywhere. The lighting was phenomenal. The sound was amazing. I had all my cues memorized, and we went over the program with everybody repeatedly. Just to make sure everyone knew their role. And maybe about the third time we reviewed *the program*, something occurred to me. This really is a production, isn't it? I didn't say that out loud, but I thought it. And not only was it a production, we'd spent a significant amount of cash to put on that production.

Now, I don't want to diminish the fact that productions can glorify God. In fact, we saw God work in phenomenal ways that day. There were hundreds of decisions. Hundreds of people raised their hands and made beautiful life-altering choices. Each church needs to discern how best to steward their resources. However, just like we Westerners sometimes have houses or cars that reflect excess, maybe our churches do too. Again, I'll cast the first stone in my direction. It's funny, no matter how lost or distracted I may feel on the inside, when it comes to the weekend services, God's Spirit always seems to redeem the moment. But still, I realized something about myself that day.

Somehow, somewhere along the line, when it came to being a pastor and leading a church, I'd put on clothes that didn't fit.

I'd done what a lot of young pastors still do. We go to the seminars that other pastors are teaching, to learn how to keep growing our churches and how to put together systems and organizational structures and strategic plans to make everything work. We start applying all these teachings and tactics. We've got to have small groups, we're told, because small groups are the secret for community and intimacy. We've got to have a certain type of preaching to attract certain kinds of people. And, we're instructed to make sure we implement some sort of formal assimilation process. Then to stay on the cutting edge, we have to launch postmodern communities, emergent gatherings, organic churches, simple churches, multiple sites, and video venues—if we are going to thrive.

So we start putting on all these clothes that fit in one cultural context but not necessarily another. We spend tons of money, rally our congregations, and have forums and town hall meetings to squeeze ourselves into a pair of tight jeans. The genius of leaders like Hybels and Warren is their ability to design new clothes that fit their contexts. Each generation of leaders is called to do the same. Our megachurch leaders get unjustly bashed by a variety of internal and external critics; it's time we relaxed and did our own thing, while affirming and celebrating the movement of God among our large churches. Sure, bigness doesn't automatically translate into success, but neither does smallness automatically equal godliness. We should concern ourselves with our own houses.

We wear these clothes, even though they don't fit, because we don't really know of any other set of clothes to wear. And it works, to a degree, because there is a genius to it. It worked with Pastor Joe; it can work for me.

And everybody says, "You look good. You look fine." But something inside you says, "It doesn't fit. Something's not right."

But if you're like me, you keep wearing them.

### My BMW

One time, after a weekend message, a leader came up to see me. He told me that something I said in the message had really resonated with him and his wife. He said that in the past two years, they'd been running really hard and really fast. They had paid off their house, which was their dream. But then for some reason, it wasn't enough. They wanted more. And they decided they needed a bigger house. And that decision, he told me, initiated a qualitative unraveling of their lives. The need to support the much bigger house with the much bigger mortgage was driving them into the ground. They were working sixty to eighty hours a week, and the bills were still piling up. They were now one million dollars in debt. He said they sat together at the service that morning and realized they were chasing after the wind. They had racked up incredible debt to support their more lavish lifestyle. He was a real-estate agent. And in my message that day I had talked about how my friends in real estate had to buy their Mercedes or their BMW to project an image of success to their clients. He told me, "Dave, when you said that, you were talking right to me, because on my desk I have a picture of a BMW I want to buy. It was my motivation to work harder."

As this young man, with his dear wife at his side, shared with me, the Holy Spirit was using him to communicate something to me. When he talked about the picture of the BMW on his desk, something inside me took root. I asked myself, "What is my BMW? What picture have I placed on my desk? What really motivates me to do the things that I do?"

In part, it was the transformation of people's lives, yes. I think that's what's in my heart. But the clothing that I had chosen to wear, that dream set of clothing, had determined the course of my life. My BMW in part was a large church, a megachurch with some high-tech goodies and hip people making a difference. Despite my good intentions, that was an important measure of my success. I'm sure other factors such as my need for acceptance and significance played into this mix as well.

Now, some unstylish people had warned me about the clothing I chose to wear, but I felt they didn't know what they were talking about. I kept running from program to program, creating new programs all the time to build a church. My rhetoric was always connected to transforming lives, but my measure of success was typically a certain type of number. (Again, numbers aren't bad by themselves, but maybe what we're counting is off.) I know I'm screwed up, but even to this day, numbers affect me. If attendance or the offering is low, God has to remind me what is important. The lure of numbers is unrelenting. And so my drivenness and my busyness kept me from seeing prayer as a priority in my life. I didn't take time to rest with God, to be in his presence, to move at his pace. I just didn't have the time. There really wasn't room for the Holy Spirit to lead the church. I was leading it. He was hitting a bottleneck called Dave Gibbons.

I finally came to an epiphany. What I needed was a new wardrobe, a closet of new clothes!

As David prepares to battle Goliath, Saul offers him his armor. Saul is afraid—for David and for himself. He asks David, "Why don't you use my armor?" But David doesn't take it. David knows he can't defeat Goliath, an adversary of a different stripe, with Saul's armor. David says, "I don't think it is going to work." Instead, David goes without armor. He chooses his own weaponry. And you know what he chooses—a sling and some stones, a crude, simple, and small choice of weapons.

David chose tools that suited him, tools that didn't seem to make sense to the "authorities" of his day. David chose offensive, not defensive, weapons. The key to David's victory was his knowledge that the source of his power wasn't Saul's high-tech equipment; it was his God.

This choice of descension is one only a true leader fully dependent on God can make. It's the kind of choice that comes from confidence in the Lord. David chose not to forget God's track record. For David it wasn't simply about numbers and metrics. His willingness to fight was based on the honor of God's name. It was about God.

You can probably sense this is a frustration for me looking back over my years in ministry. I just kept growing this thing. I kept building a bigger worship experience, a bigger place, where it was easy for people to think they were growing spiritually. Though most of us in ministry are motivated to reach as many people for Jesus as possible, the problem comes when we measure our success simply by the numbers, when we think ministry has to take this specific form to have the greatest influence.

But I had to come to grips with a set of questions: Were people's lives any different? Were the city and community really being transformed? Were hurt and pain really being addressed with the marginalized in our community? Were people becoming David-like in their obedience and faith? Were we forging real and stronger relationships with people who are not like us?

## New Bottom Lines

I've had the opportunity to travel to some twenty different countries in the past twenty-four months. Going to these places—places like Thailand, India, Mexico, the United Kingdom, where we are starting churches and helping indigenous people with social justice efforts—has opened my eyes to the many unhealthy thoughts and practices I'd embraced as a pastor without ever knowing it. Default ways of thinking about and doing church and ministry that I believe led me down a destructive road.

One time on a trip to Thailand—where we have a young church and social justice endeavors—I met with this career Christian missionary who was talking about the despair of the Christian worker in Thailand. Christian missionaries have been in this beautiful country for more than a hundred and twenty-five years. And yet, he told me, they haven't been able to reach more than one percent of the country's sixty-one million people. And I wondered, Why? Why is it still less than one percent?

Then I visited one of the international churches in Thailand and saw that there were hardly any Thai people there. That really struck me. Actually, I got dismayed about it. And I thought, "Why are Christian missionaries here in the first place? Why create a church in this land if they're not reaching out to the Thai people?" How are we being international if we're not making a significant difference among the local people groups?

I'm convinced we need new metrics, new ways to measure and define success—for our own sake and for the sake of the people we're trying to reach with God's love.

God says to Abraham, "I'm going to make you the father of many, the father of multitudes." There are numbers in the Bible about how many people were saved. And there are passages in Revelation and Isaiah about all the nations coming together. So obviously God cares about numbers. But what he counts is different. In the passages where numbers are very much a part of the story, what God cares most about is the transformation—of lives and of the world he created—and the relationships that are reflected in those numbers.

What we idolize today, I think, is a form of church and ministry that revolves around bigness.

### Small Is the New Big

While I was in Vietnam, I learned the unique power of the small.

Some of our leaders and I visited the Cu-Chi Tunnels outside of Saigon in Vietnam. This is an underground network of tunnels that the Vietnamese farmers built when the Americans were dropping napalm bombs during the Vietnam War.

No matter what you believe about the ethical nature of the war, what's interesting is how the Vietnamese survived. These agrarian people, who didn't have weapons other than simple farm instruments, withstood all the machinery and military muscle of this mighty nation called America. And they did more than withstand; they demoralized the American military and the American people. How did they do it? They worked in small units. Small units led by women. And though they were small, they were powerful. They converted parts from the military machines that fell from the sky and used them for their own defense. They reengineered them to be their tools.

Think about 9/11. A small band of terrorists have caused all kinds of disruption not only in America but around the world. Billions of dollars are spent on security and defense today that weren't being spent on September 10, 2001. And think about how much the level of fear and insecurity has increased because of the small group of terrorists that acted on that day. They have a bold mantra too, given their size. They say, "If you knock me out, a thousand more will rise up to take my place." And they say it with conviction.

In his book *Small Giants*, author Bo Burlingame looks at the rapidly changing business world and talks about companies that are making names for themselves and having a huge influence because they choose to be small. Because they are small, they are free to be what's important to them and their leaders.

When I think about all of these things, I can't help but think of another tiny group of people some two thousand years ago. Jesus and his twelve misfit followers weren't much to look at. They were hardly a scary number. It would have been easy to underestimate their potential. Yet they launched a movement far greater than what anybody, even they themselves, ever imagined. Jesus spent the majority of his time simply walking with these men. Me? I cannot begin to tell you how many days, weeks, and months I've spent in church and ministry thinking about growth mechanisms and organizational scaling strategies and retention tactics and so on. Now I find myself trying not to "lead" the congregation but more importantly to support them and ascertain how I can fan the flames of their leadership. Our staff is the support team. The members are the field team.

### A New Metric: The Metric of Embrace

Miroslav Volf, a brilliant theologian and professor at Yale University Divinity School, writes,

> An embrace involves always a double movement of opening and closing. I open my arms to create space in myself for the other. The open arms are a sign of discontent at being myself only and of desire to include the other. They are an invitation to the others to come in and feel at home with me, to belong to me. In an embrace I also close my arms around the others—not tightly, so as to crush and assimilate them forcefully into myself, for that would not be an embrace but a concealed power-act of exclusion; but gently, so as to tell them that I do not want to be without them in their otherness. I want them to remain independent and true to their genuine selves, to maintain their identity and as such become part of me so that they can enrich me with what they have and I do not.[4]

This is the metric of embrace. We know in our hearts whether we embrace someone or exclude them from the inner sanctums of our lives. Objectively, how many people who are from a different culture than us do we include in our lives? How much time do we spend developing relationships across cultural or socio-economic differences to demonstrate the gospel message of loving God and loving our neighbor?

One way you can find out how you're doing with this metric is to ask the communities near your church that are different from you if they feel you are loving them with sacrificial, radical love. These communities can be social agencies, community-development groups, or churches already serving in ethnic or underresourced communities. They can give you an honest evaluation.

Another great way to measure how well you embrace other cultures is to ask yourself how often you eat cultural food you don't like. This may sound crazy to you, but nothing represents the soul of a culture more than her food. Trying ethnic food is a foray into culture. Just taking the initiative to eat another person's type of ethnic food with them can be quite an obstacle for some. Eating kimchee or chicken feet can be a test of your embrace. Eating someone's ethnic food with them is a tangible way to do life with them, a demonstration that you're trying to be one with them. (And try to do it without looking like you're taking cough medicine!) Perhaps this is what communion is about. The epitome of our relationship with the "other," or someone who is like us and totally *not* like us, is our relationship with Jesus. To know him is to eat with him: communion. There is something mystical, spiritual that happens when we eat with Jesus. It links hearts and minds. What better way to know people than eating, drinking, laughing, listening, remembering, and sharing with them around a table or while sitting on the floor?

The pursuit of this metric of embrace is not easy because it's relational. For Volf, it meant loving the *cetniks*, Serbian fighters who had been "sowing desolation" in his native country, "herding people into concentration camps, raping women, burning down churches, and destroying cities."[5] To him, this was the neighbor, the ultimate other, and it meant wearing a set of clothes he didn't want to wear. But he put them on.

Loving the other can be messy, ugly, unnatural, and perhaps not fun, but this is the set of clothes we all have been called to wear. And one size fits all who know Jesus.

# Neighbor

The Bible is very easy to understand. But we Christians are a bunch of scheming swindlers. We pretend to be unable to understand it because we know very well that the minute we understand, we are obliged to act accordingly.

—Søren Kierkegaard

Ubuntu is a concept that we have in our Bantu languages at home. Ubuntu is the essence of being a person. It means that we are people through other people. We cannot be fully human alone. We are made for interdependence, we are made for family. When you have ubuntu, you embrace others. You are generous, compassionate. If the world had more ubuntu, we would not have war. We would not have this huge gap between the rich and the poor. You are rich so that you can make up what is lacking for others. You are powerful so that you can help the weak, just as a mother or father helps their children. This is God's dream.

—Desmond Tutu, *God Has a Dream*

One of the axioms I've come to believe about life and ministry is that questions should lead us. Questions, not answers.

Jesus showed us this time and again. But for some reason we forget. We think we have to have all the answers, as Christians and church leaders. And worse yet, we sometimes think we actually do have all the answers. Or at least our actions are such that people around the world perceive us that way. I've certainly been guilty of this.

The Scriptures recount a moment when a religious expert asks Jesus, "What must I do to inherit eternal life?" Jesus responds with a question of his own. He asks the man, "What is written in the law? How do you read it?"

The man answers, " 'Love the Lord your God with all your heart and with all your soul and with all your strength and with all your mind'; and, 'Love your neighbor as yourself.' "

"Right!" Jesus tells him. "Do this and you will live."

This seems like an important enough truth in and of itself and a tall order—love God and love your neighbor. But the story goes on.

The Scriptures say the religious expert wants to justify his actions, so he asks Jesus, "And who is my neighbor?"

If Jesus doesn't answer a question with a question, he usually answers it with a story. In this case, the story Jesus tells is one of the most recognized in the entire Bible—the story of the good Samaritan.

I think this story is perhaps one of the most misunderstood in all of the Scriptures. I also think, in today's world, the meaning of this story may be one of the most critical truths for those of us laboring on behalf of the radical love contained in the gospel to comprehend.

In the story of the good Samaritan, Jesus recounts that a Jewish man is traveling from Jerusalem to Jericho. The man is attacked by bandits. The attackers strip him of his clothing, snatch his money, beat him up, and leave him half dead beside the road.

By chance, Jesus says, a Jewish priest comes along. The Jewish priest sees the Jewish man bloodied and suffering and lying helplessly on the roadside. But instead of coming to the man's aid, the priest crosses to the other side of the road and walks by, probably hurriedly.

A second person walks along the same path, a temple assistant. The temple assistant, Jesus says, actually walks over and looks at the injured man, but he too chooses to pass by on the other side without helping him.

A third person, Jesus says, walks by—a Samaritan, an ethnicity that was despised by the Jewish people at the time. When the Samaritan sees the hurt Jewish man, Jesus says the Samaritan feels pity and empathy. His compassion supercedes the sociocultural taboos of his day.

The Samaritan kneels beside the man and gently gives him aid. Jesus says the Samaritan soothes the man's wounds with medicine and bandages him. Then the Samaritan puts the Jewish man on his own donkey and takes him to an inn.

The Samaritan spends the night with the man in the inn. The next day he hands the innkeeper enough money to provide for the man's stay and tells him to take care of the man. "If his bill runs higher than that," the Samaritan says, "I'll pay the difference the next time I am here."

Then Jesus asks the religious leader, "Now, which of these three would you say was a neighbor to the man who was attacked by bandits?"

The religious expert replies, "The one who showed him mercy."

"Precisely," Jesus says. "So go and do likewise."

I don't know how many times I've heard this story, studied it, and listened to it recounted in church. And I was always told that its primary meaning is that I am to be kind to my neighbor, and that my neighbor is somebody who is basically a lot like me but in need in some way.

While in ministry, I learned that this interpretation of Jesus' story had become the basis for growing churches. A brilliant missiologist named Donald McGavran came up with an important concept known as the homogeneous principle.[6] The homogeneous principle basically states that people are willing to come together based on their similarities. McGavran wanted to demonstrate that we shouldn't be insular or exclusive in our approach. However, other proponents of church-growth shared through books and seminars how churches could grow rapidly using this principle of likes attracting. So for most of my years as a pastor, I viewed my neighbor as somebody like me—an Asian/white, middle-class suburbanite.

Then the Medici effect happened. The Medici effect happens when you're at a place of multiple cultural intersections, where learning and innovation are heightened. During a season of my life, I was able to visit or live in places like Thailand, India, Vietnam, Latin America, China, London, Mexico City, and El Salvador. This season was magical to me. It was a gift, a beautiful journey into Thailand, where my family and I lived for about one year. At a time when our church in America was having its highest attendance numbers and our multisites were bigger than they had ever been, we felt God calling us to learn from and be with the people of Thailand. People said we were crazy, but I think it saved my life and opened my eyes to the supernatural power of God and his love for people. This was a Narnia-like time for me, when I not only discovered my illusions of God, myself, others, and my work but also discovered what and who are real. We saw miracles and we saw great heartaches. Yet I found purpose, and more important, I felt God's presence and power again. The two greatest commandments reemerged for examination and contemplation: love God with all your heart, soul, and mind, and love your neighbor as yourself.

So who is my neighbor?

I had approached building Newsong based on the idea that my neighbor is someone like me. But as I dug into Luke 10 with fresh eyes, I saw things from the persepective of someone who lives outside of America. For the first time I realized that when this young religious leader asked Jesus who his neighbor was, Jesus responded with a story. Just doing that—answering his question with a story—is such an Eastern thing to do. You see, in the Eastern world, and especially in Asia, life is all about nuance. Often an answer is given not directly but indirectly. It's part of the culture that when someone asks a question, you don't answer dogmatically. You don't pound answers into people.

While we in the Western tradition may not have completely grasped Jesus' point in this story, a person from the Eastern and Middle Eastern parts of the world in Jesus' day would have understood his message clearly. The neighbor is the good Samaritan, a person of mixed descent—half-Jew and half-Gentile. Much to the dismay of Jesus' Jewish audience, the hero of the story is a person they despised. Jesus was telling the religious leader that his neighbor, instead of being someone like him, was someone not like him at all, someone he would be uncomfortable with or even hate.

This is what has become so clear to me. The second most important commandment is all about loving people we don't understand, whom maybe even the community we live in doesn't like, maybe even hates, or at the least disregards or writes off. People who are misfits. People who are marginalized. People who are outsiders. Loving my neighbor is not about likenesses at all. It's not about people who happen to share my skin color or ethnicity, or about people who talk like me and think like me, people who like the same food as me and like the same things I do. Instead, it's about people I would not normally choose to befriend, people who might make me feel uncomfortable to be around.

This is true in my life and in the life of the church, it may very well mean that the church doesn't grow numerically nearly as quickly as it otherwise might. But doing this—loving people who are unlike us and who are not necessarily accepted or understood by our own community or culture — is absolutely doing the work and will of Christ. It's at the heart of fulfilling the intent of the second greatest commandment. It's a taste of something extraordinarily unusual, so different from the normal rhythm of humanity that it causes people to take a second look or to pause and listen because it strikes them as something supernatural.

What's interesting is that the more I reflect on these two commandments, the more I realize they are inseparable. They're two sides of the same coin. To love someone who is outside my comfort zone, someone I would not naturally be attracted to, is actually loving God.

Jesus says, "If you love the least of these, you have loved me." Then there's 1 John, where the apostle John, who was fittingly called John the Beloved, writes that if you can't love people whom you can see, how can you love God, whom you can't see? Whoever loves God has to love his brother too.

So if this interpretation of the second greatest commandment is true, what does it mean for the way we do church? What does it mean for how we measure success?

Well, it changes everything.

## Theology of Discomfort

Throughout the 1980s and '90s, we in the church not only spent a lot of time, bandwidth, and focus trying to create places that attract people just like us, we also worked hard at making church comfortable and convenient. We became really good at producing large-screen extravaganzas that rival network television, complete with cutting-edge programming, free donuts, cushy seating, welcome teams, parking, free wireless, and ATMs in the foyer. (How could we have missed this one?) And we've filled our rooms and sanctuaries with people who look, think, and act just like one another. While we speak of loving our neighbors, we usually mean the people in our geographical neighborhood who are just like us.

We started espousing this comfortology en masse about two decades ago, largely because of the church-growth strategy that sprang from the homogeneous principle. That principle basically birthed the church-growth movement in America and in other parts of the world.

(Interestingly, I met a student of Dr. McGavran's who had traveled with him, rooming with him on their trips. He shared that although McGavran popularized the homogeneous principle, it wasn't necessarily to support the church-growth movement specifically but more to warn the church of its natural tendency to stay within its own culture. Dr. McGavran's well-known statement is that people "like to become Christians without crossing racial, linguistic, or class barriers."[7] He added that McGavran had a heart for the world.)

Although I know firsthand that the homogeneous principle works, it has always bothered me, especially as leaders applied it to the demographic they were trying to reach. But not until recent years—as I've watched the world dramatically change—have I been able to put my finger on the source of this nagging disequilibrium in my spirit.

While we've poured our resources into perfecting strategies to create church bubbles of homogeneous people, the colorful communities that have quietly sprung up around our churches and neighborhoods are anything but homogeneous.

As I write, I'm sitting in a coffee shop in Irvine, a place that just ten years ago was predominantly white, middle class, conservative, and Christian. It's a microcosm of how the world is being reshaped. Forty percent of Irvine's population is made up of Chinese, Korean, Japanese, Indian, Latino, and Vietnamese people. Sitting at the table to my right are six Latino women talking in Spanish. Two Korean college students are hard at work at a table by the door. Two Chinese high school students are studying for finals right in front of me. A Japanese businessman clicks away at his laptop right behind me. And an elegant Indian woman, head covered in a cream silk scarf, has just walked in to order a latte.

Even in remote Midwestern towns you find people from India, Laos, Vietnam, Korea, Africa, Mexico, Latin America, the Middle East, China, Australia, and many other countries.

In my neighborhood, it is a veritable United Nations.

Take a close look at who's sitting in the classrooms of your local elementary school or in your local restaurants. Our neighbors—yours and mine—have radically changed, but our focus hasn't.

Is it possible that we in the church are called to be radically different in how we think about and act toward those the Bible would define as our neighbors, even at the cost of losing members? What if we became arithmetically smaller yet stronger bands of wild-eyed zealots who embrace the life that Jesus did, a life that is frequently about discomfort, a life that is all about a radical new view of who a neighbor is—someone of a different culture whom you may even hate?

If any word epitomizes Jesus' life, it's discomfort, from the beginning—his birth amid poverty, in a bed of straw, into a hostile world—to the end—his death, by the Via Dolorosa, full of shame, sacrifice, humility, pain, betrayal, and rejection.

Embracing a life of discomfort means venturing into places we don't feel like going, doing things we don't wish to do, being with people we don't feel comfortable being with, serving them, loving them, helping them—all of which demonstrates a not-of-this-world brand of love that is irresistible to all people in all places.

If we do these sorts of things in our churches, we generally relegate them to the missions or local outreach departments. Churchwide, we might embrace these kinds of elements with, at best, a choir exchange with the African-American church down the road or a weekend highlighting disadvantaged youth. That, if we're honest, tends to be the extent of our comfort zone.

In the world we now live in, the single best thing a church can be doing today is contrary to the homogeneous principle. It means rallying behind kingdom values and vision, rather than skin color and socio-economic status. It means recognizing we are called to wrestle with deeper questions: Are we intentionally including people in our lives that make us uncomfortable? Are we spending time with, and pouring our lives out for, people who make us uncomfortable?

Here's the reality: if we really want to see our churches grow in the way Jesus would want us to grow, if we really want to see Christ revealed in our communities and through our lives and in this global world of ours, then we must focus our strategic initiatives of love on people who make us feel uncomfortable, who don't fit into our thinking and our conventions, who are marginalized and even considered misfits and outsiders.

Individual churches might not grow as quickly, but I believe with all of my heart that the Church would be more enduring and virile and robust and alive than ever. We would meet Jesus in more compelling ways than ever before. We would reflect the true nature and character of Jesus.

When the world sees the church willing to forego size and scale to love and embrace people who are not like us, treating them as neighbors, they can sense an expression of true and genuine love. It's a thing of miraculous beauty. And people know beauty when they see it.

Anyone can love people who are like themselves. The Father's love is best reflected—and is most irresistible and potent—when we love those who are unattractive to us. So when we make that our priority, people outside the church start to see God in all his fullness. There's something truly divine about a movement of people who reach out to love others and be with others whom they find difficult to understand or love or be with.

But when we allow our churches to be mostly homogeneous, we tend to do things that are comfortable to us. We focus on conceiving and executing programs and events that attract more people just like us, which often is more Christians looking for another church that meets their needs.

The gospel is about so much more, isn't it?

The soul of the Great Commission and the Great Commandment leans into difficult people and their complexities. It's to be the essence of who we are as Christians. In fact, unity of mind and generosity of spirit in the midst of diversity is the distinguishing mark of true Christian community.

It's a bold, radical endeavor: to love our neighbor. But it's the endeavor God has called us to. It's where the gospel becomes real. It really speaks to the power of Jesus if we can work through our discomfort and overcome the barriers we too easily let divide us.

This concept, this theology of discomfort, can be seen throughout the Scriptures, both in the Old and New Testaments. So much so it makes me realize how often we can know what is right but practice what is merely expedient.

Throughout the Old Testament we hear that we are to radically love outsiders, widows, and orphans, to act as a voice for the voiceless, and to be a father to the fatherless. In Corinthians we see God saying he focuses on the weak of this world to speak to the mighty. In John 14, Jesus explains to the disciples that obeying him and loving the "least of these" in society give us deep understanding about him and his ways.

In Acts 8, there's an odd but revealing story involving an Ethiopian eunuch. At first, you might wonder about the meaning of this story, but I think it speaks beautifully of the theology of discomfort, especially as it pertains to misfits or outcasts. If anyone ranked as a misfit or outcast in the first-century world, it would be a eunuch. Eunuchs had access to the powerful and privileged, because kings and emperors weren't worried about them messing around with their wives and harems. But nobody reaped more scorn and ridicule. The elite in society likened eunuchs to a dry root, someone who had been cut off from the main branches of society. A eunuch didn't merit recognition or acknowledgment, and certainly not much respect or attention.

In the Acts 8 account, the Ethiopian eunuch had gone to Jerusalem to find God. But when he got to the temple, he wasn't allowed in by the priests because Deuteronomy bars eunuchs from the temple. So the eunuch heads back to his country. He's broken. He is physically and spiritually cut off.

But what does God do? He sends Philip, the apostle of Jesus, to tell the eunuch there's another one who also has been cut off, who also has been rejected, and his name is Jesus. And the Ethiopian eunuch basically says in disbelief, "You mean there is someone like *me*?" Philip goes on to tell him about Jesus.

Now, we don't know all the details of their encounter and conversation but we can make some inferences, based on what we know about the culture at that time. As he listened to Philip talk about Jesus, it's likely the eunuch, who probably was familiar with the Old Testament scrolls, recalled that in Isaiah God says there will come a day when the Messiah returns and eunuchs will become better than sons or daughters. It likely was a source of wonder and joy to the eunuch to connect this prophecy to Jesus, whom Philip undoubtedly identified as the long-awaited Messiah.

And what of Jesus himself and this notion of misfits and outcasts and neighbors? Well, time and again in the Gospels,

Jesus chooses to be identified with people who are on the outside looking in, those whom most people of his day felt uncomfortable being around and justified in ignoring. People who had messed up, people branded as outsiders—they all felt like insiders around Jesus, like they finally belonged somewhere.

In his insightful book *Velvet Elvis*, Rob Bell, an incredible communicator and pastor of a vibrant, thriving church in the Midwest, reveals just how unlikely it was that Jesus chose the disciples he did.

In first-century Jewish culture, rabbis started weeding out the best potential students at age six. By the time a boy was thirteen or fourteen, he got pegged as either having it or not. The boys with the most potential—those who had memorized as many of the thirty-nine books of the Torah as possible—had the chance to become followers of the rabbis.

If a potential student passed a rabbi's rigorous screening, the rabbi would ask the student to "come and follow me." The student would then leave family, the village, the synagogue, and much of what was familiar to him to follow the rabbi. He would shadow the rabbi everywhere and basically become just like the rabbi.

If the rabbi didn't feel the student was the best of the best, he sent him home to the family business or to learn a common trade, like fishing. A rabbi wasn't going to waste his time with a youth who didn't have it.

That's why it was so revolutionary and so radical when the Rabbi of rabbis came on the scene. Jesus looked at a bunch of fishermen—a bunch of other rabbis' rejects—and saw in them something most people wouldn't see. Instead of asking the best of the best to come and follow him, Jesus challenged a motley crew of young fishermen to be his followers. And remember, it's likely that these were boys fourteen to sixteen years old. That's who Jesus chose!

One of the many things that's so striking about this, as Rob Bell points out, is that we often talk to people about believing in Jesus, having faith in Jesus. But how about turning that around: Jesus believes in *you*. Jesus has faith in *you*. The Rabbi of rabbis thinks *we* can become like him!

This is countercultural and revolutionary. This is the type of church and kingdom I want to be a part of—a band of people who are messy, have addictions and shortcomings, make mistakes, get rejected, and are screwed up, but are so fully aware of the Master's grace and love for them in spite of who they are or once were or will be someday; people who embrace discomfort knowing there is so much to be gained for all of us and for all of our churches. How? In passionately pursuing a biblical love for those whom the Bible defines as a neighbor. Especially today. It's a time in history when technology and global cultural shifts have made neighbors of all of us. We are surrounded by people of vastly different and unfamiliar cultures, beliefs, and backgrounds. Our neighborhoods are buzzing with new cultural sights, smells, and sounds and a dynamism fueled by immigration and the fusion of ethnic people groups. The recent census reminds us that minorities in America will soon become the majority. With this population shift, new outsiders will emerge, modern-day eunuchs who are cut off. This is the time when a third-culture church shines.

## Squishing Room Only

Not long ago I received a very cool email from one of the leaders of the church we started in Bangkok. Bangkok is one of the places where I've been learning so much in practical terms about this biblical notion of who my neighbor is in today's world. In the email, the leader makes reference to a Saturday night "verge." Again, this is the term we use for our midsize informal gatherings, and the verges seem popular in all of the places we've started churches, in part because they seem to draw an incredibly diverse group of people, whether in London, Mexico City, or, in this instance, Bangkok.

> This weekend on Saturday there wasn't even standing room enough for everyone. It got to the point where there was squishing room only! When you go to the Saturday verge, you need to sit with people you know well cuz you end up leaning on everyone around you, elbows here, knees there.
>
> Every weekend at least one person tells me they have been searching for "this" or been praying to find a place "like this."
>
> Dave, you might remember Justin, the young guy I introduced to you. He's had lots of questions and I've really been challenging his old paradigm of evangelism and missions. Lots of talks and encouraging him not to be afraid of "the world" and to take Jesus with him into everyday life instead of believing that bringing people to church is the same as bringing them to Jesus.

So this past Saturday, I was sitting near the door, and during the worship, a young woman squishes in and sits next to me on the arm of the sofa. Then another girl squishes in front of her on the arm of the sofa. Just picture three of us on the one arm of this sofa! Then Justin squishes in through the door and stands there, eyes bright and a smile on his face. He yells into my ear above the music, "You wouldn't believe the story I have to tell you!"

Afterward he explained to me how these two girls are prostitutes, how his colleague thought it might be funny to hook this innocent young Christian guy up with them, and poor Justin didn't even know at the time. He naturally brought them to Newsong, cuz he was on his way there, and he knew no one could feel out of place there. They came along. They got to hear about the Father's love.

This is a bit of a funny story, in a way, but a story about Justin's journey as well as these two bar girls. Misfits. All of us.

From my perch on the arm of the sofa, I kept looking around the room all evening. Thais. Koreans. Americans. Teachers. Computer experts. Designers. Bar girls. Musicians. Peaceful faces. Pained faces. Even some tell-me-something-I-don't-know faces. Everything and everyone so distinct and different.

We don't have Pastor Big Name. We don't have Pastor Big Microphone. We don't have Cathedral on the Corner. We have people in shorts filling in and taking turns speaking. We have humble who-is-he-again? leading worship. We have crooked stairs and a back door that serves as our

> front door. We have mismatched chairs and floor pillows, yellow walls and no doorknobs. Barebones skinny.
>
> But God is decorating that place with himself! People gathered in his name are promised to see him lifted up among them. We are seeing him lifted up. He is showing himself to be great.

We are to be the living extension of Jesus' hands and heart to the world. And with what's happening in the world today, if we live out a theology of discomfort and embrace a biblical definition of who our neighbors are in our churches, both in America and abroad, then we are loving the neighbor Jesus defined two thousand years ago. A neighbor totally unlike us.

# Liquid Bruce Lee

> Rescuing God from religion is how I'd put it. All these rules and regulations and locked doors keep God a prisoner who cannot be shared unless we do this, that, or the other.
>
> —Sinead O'Connor

> I distrust those people who know so well what God wants them to do, because I know it always coincides with their own desires.
>
> —Susan B. Anthony

You're probably going to wonder where I'm headed with this, but to make a point about how doing church and ministry in the age of globalism is very different from what we're used to, think kiwi.

The kiwi is this fuzzy, moist, succulent fruit. It's originally from New Zealand and used to be something that mainly New Zealanders got to enjoy. But by the mid-1980s, the kiwi had become a worldwide product people loved.

You could see commercials and advertisements about the kiwi just about anyplace in the world. It had grown into a 2.5 billion dollars a year industry. That's really pretty amazing for a piece of fruit. In comparison, the Hollywood movie industry is about a ten billion dollars a year industry. So the kiwi is right up there.

Besides the financial angle, the kiwi was a highly successful national symbol for New Zealand. It had become the economic and cultural foundation for an entire nation. It helped fuel a highly lucrative travel and tourism industry in New Zealand. New Zealanders even came to be known as Kiwis.

In short, New Zealand had become the kiwi capital of the planet. If you wanted to buy kiwis, then you had to do business with New Zealand, which was the world's exclusive kiwi exporter throughout the 1970s and '80s, when the kiwi market came of age.

Then, seemingly overnight, something happened.

By the early 1990s, kiwi growers began springing up in other nations, such as South Africa, Chile, France, Italy, and Spain, and began taking bites out of the kiwi market. They posed a threat not only to New Zealand's economy but also to its culture and identity.

I don't want to oversimplify it, but some people in New Zealand's government and industry realized they needed to figure out what to do in response or things were going to get out of hand pretty quickly. They teamed up people in business, government, and culture to figure out new ways of operating. They recognized the world had changed. They didn't know what new strategies to embrace, but they did know they wanted to continue to enjoy the benefits the kiwi gave their economy, culture, and nation. They ended up tapping into some pretty novel horticultural science and technology. They started some new partnerships and collaborations. And they started doing things differently.

How so? Well, today you can get kiwis that don't look like a traditional kiwi or taste like a traditional kiwi. You can get the kiwi in a variety of colors, not just the traditional green. You can get them with different ranges of tang and sweetness. You can also get these new kiwis from new places around the world, such as Japan, Korea, and even the United States, because the New Zealand farmers and producers had the foresight to grant collaborative licenses to people who otherwise would have become competitors.

The results have been pretty stellar. The new versions of the kiwi have helped reinvigorate New Zealand's standing as possessor of the planet's preeminent kiwi crops.

Now, I'm fascinated by stories of change and innovation, especially success stories. Because change is hard. And it's getting even harder to change because it has to be done faster and on a global scale.

If you are fortunate enough to talk to anyone in the New Zealand kiwi business, they can fill your ears with stories about how a relatively simple business—growing and selling the world's favorite fuzzy fruit—has been absolutely jolted by the forces of globalism.

They can tell you they discovered they had to look at the world and at themselves in a whole new way.

They can tell you that what were once occasional, fairly predictable gusts of change developed into permanent, hurricane-force winds.

They can point to the wild pace and large scale of the exchange of ideas, information, and insight that is taking place 24/7 across 1.5 million miles of fiber-optic cable now connecting every continent on earth.

They can tell you they've learned that, more than ever, complacency is lethal.

They can tell you there is no guarantee that what has worked in the past will work today in a new generation and in a new world of information superhighways linking nations, cultures, and people like never before.

They can also tell you that all of their efforts, which began with a crisis, resulted in a fruit that, though it looks different, tastes different, and even comes from a different place, is still a kiwi.

Just about every day a headline proclaims another example of how globalism and technology are impacting institutions, industries, organizations, and domains. It can be overwhelming, really. But I believe that those of us in the church and in ministry can learn a lot from this one ultra-simple example of the kiwi.

We must be about something that's fundamentally meaningful to others. Just because it's high on our agenda and works in the American megachurch doesn't mean it has value in a rapidly changing world.

Each generation must create a new language that connects with the soul and life of their community in their era. It must also create new forms not only to help carry the message, the truth, the content into a new generation but also to create a greater hunger for that message. So while the message may stay the same, the forms do change. Jesus himself modeled this; the Word, which had always been, became flesh. The message came in a new form, in the form of a messenger. Why? So that we may touch him, see him, and experience him and, by doing so, may truly understand the ancient, eternal message of God's love.

Today we in the church must enter unfamiliar and even dangerous terrain, perhaps even taking on fears we never imagined ourselves confronting. If somebody in the kiwi biz had suggested to his bosses during the heyday that they should consider changing the color of the kiwi, they'd probably find themselves looking at an interesting color themselves—a pink slip!

We really do need to partner with previously unthinkable partners and do so in previously inconceivable ways. I don't know about you, but I get absolutely inspired when I think about how this one change—looking at people around the world as a resource for partnerships—might alter how we do ministry and translate the gospel around our world. It's like seeing the gifts of the Holy Spirit pertaining not just to one local church but to the whole global church. Could not the members of the church also be nations or people groups? For the church to be at its best, one culture's gifts matter. We need each other's gifts to make the greatest difference and to be the greatest expression of Christ on earth.

It's critical for us to grasp the need for change and to act on it. It isn't just about whether we can maintain our numbers. It's about maintaining our identity and our ability to influence the world in this new era.

Just like the kiwi, the church needs to look different, feel different, taste different, sound different, be different to the people in our churches and the people we hope will be in our churches.

Same mission.

Same dream.

Same truth.

Same message.

Yet new forms.

New languages.

New containers.

New priests and messengers.

New relationships.

## The Art of Being Water

Bruce Lee, the legendary martial arts star, might rank as my all-time favorite hero. When I was growing up in what was mostly an Anglo and Mexican neighborhood in Arizona, people constantly called me Bruce Lee. It had nothing to do with my martial arts skills, I can assure you. It was because I was Asian-American. People at that time assumed that all Asians had black belts and had been trained by senseis since the age of two. How hilarious! If you knew me, you'd know in a second that fighting's not my thing. I'm one of those lover-not-a-fighter types.

But Bruce Lee wasn't just a fighter either. He had a philosophical bent. In an interview, Lee explained his philosophy about life and his craft in this unique way: "You put water into a cup, it becomes the cup. You put water into the bottle, it becomes the bottle. You put it into a teapot and it becomes a teapot. The water can flow. The water can crash. Be water, my friend."[8]

I could be wrong, but I'm not sure there's a better piece of counsel for us in the church today. Our task as the church is to be water. To flow. Not crash.

Our water — our message — remains what it always has been: the love of Jesus. Our forms, our containers, can change. Must change. Furthermore, our conflicts shouldn't be about forms. It's a waste of our energy. Whether it's music, terminology, preaching, graphics, size, buildings, arbitrary legalistic rules, clothes, who cares? I could be wrong about this too, but I have a hard time imagining that God cares much about these crazy conflicts about forms.

Being third culture is about being water to a world that is deeply thirsty when it comes to spirituality and meaning, and is in need of adaptive and contextualized language and forms when talking about God and Christianity.

We're learning at our different Newsong locations around the world that we need to be open to creatively designing or embracing new forms, languages, customs, and containers to deliver that water.

This mindset — a passion to be open to new cultures and new ways, and a devotion to see shifts in society and the world at large and to respond exuberantly and artfully — is at the heart of being a third-culture church.

## Shifts That Mark Third-Culture Churches

### *From Consumerism to Cause-ism*

There's a pretty well-known safe house in Southern California that provides sanctuary for runaways and troubled teenagers. If on any weekend you happen to swing by the house, you can catch a glimpse of how much things are changing in our culture and specifically within the younger generation. What you'd likely see is a bunch of teenagers holding what looks like one of those neighborhood car washes that typical high schoolers all across America hold. Usually it's to benefit their athletic departments or cheerleading squads or whatever other program may be in need. The kids at the safe house may look a little shaggier than most, but otherwise they wave their banners and wield sudsy sponges and slippery water hoses with the best of them.

While the scene looks quite common, it's anything but. The troubled teenagers at the safe house, you see, wash cars not to meet any of their own substantial needs but to raise money to help African children left orphaned and wounded by the genocide and civil war in Sudan.

Think about that for a minute. A bunch of teenagers struggling with drugs and hardships and modern life in general are not only aware of the details of a tragedy happening on the other side of the globe but also have decided on their own to do something about it. And the technology exists for them to give legs to their yearning to do good.

What's further intriguing and instructive for us is that a church in Southern California recently approached the safe house to say that their congregation had decided that they wanted to help the kids there. The church knew nothing of the safe house's outreach to the Sudanese children. What they heard back from them took them aback: "Thanks for the offer, but if you want to help us, we'd rather you just help the kids in Sudan."

That's third culture. They are focused on loving someone different from them not only ethnically but socio-economically.

If we're honest, we often feel pretty good about ourselves and our churches if we have a ministry that does something to serve needy people in our communities. And if we're still keeping it real, we also usually do this with our own agenda—religious conversion. Conversely, the kids at the safe house harbor no agenda other than goodwill and a dream, a wish, to help children who can't help themselves. That's love without a single strand of string attached to it.

We're learning that our churches and ministries need to be about this brand of undiluted compassion. It's one of the guiding principles of what we're calling a third-culture church—to love without strings.

Our message and our motivation simply cannot be anything like a multilevel marketing presentation.

I wonder if you've ever had something like this happen to you. Not long ago I attended a seminar for church leaders. An energetic young man approached and befriended me. "What a friendly guy," I thought to myself. He then asked if I was interested in global investment. "Oh yeah. I'm into it," I told him. He then invited me to a session he was doing on the topic, assuring me I'd love it. I promised I'd be there and looked forward to learning about and discussing one of my favorite subjects. Part of my rationale for going was that we were at a ministry conference, he seemed like a nice guy, and he seemed to care about me and my interests and my future.

Well, when I showed up at the meeting, I was one of about fifty people there. He couldn't take the time to even say hello to me, and then he started out on the seminar. What did it turn out to be? You've probably already guessed. He introduced a way for us to make money by selling products and recruiting others to sell on our behalf. Yeah. One of those direct-marketing, pyramid-scheme things.

I hightailed it out of there angry that this guy had really shamed me and made me feel like a fool. I went home and started to write a letter to him about how he had befriended me not because he cared for me but because I was a potential down-line for him.

As I reflected on how much this affected me, it occurred to me that too often we in the church do similar things. All of a sudden I had a pretty good idea how it must feel to people.

What makes this story about the safe house and the Sudanese outreach all the more pertinent for us today is that there's an awakening happening in the next generation around the world. And we in the church may want to take note. If we're not careful, I fear we'll become known for a love with hidden conditions, while much of the world around us—like the safe house kids—reaches out to help people in need with purer, nobler motives. What's happened is that technology and 24/7 news cycles have created unprecedented awareness of the myriad injustices taking place on this troubled planet. This awareness has impacted every secular realm of society, including politics, business, education, and entertainment. Being socially responsible—and doing so for the right reasons—has taken on a whole new emphasis.

The challenge is that we in the church for a long time now have tried to cater to the "customer" in our pews, trying to make church as convenient as possible because we know how busy people are and how fractured their attention span is. We've aimed our resources, ministries, and programs at making church as simple and fun and easy as possible.

Much good has flowed from this way of thinking and operating and will continue to do so. But I wonder if we haven't unwittingly created organisms that are unhealthy to ourselves and to others, organizations that are uninspiring to the world. It's like creating something meant for good, but before you know it, it has veered in an unintended direction and become a negative force.

Are there different ways of doing church? Ways that seem better suited for our times? Ways that would put the church in the best possible position to do the most good for the sake of the gospel?

Half a world away, while living in Bangkok, freed from biases and assumptions that have influenced me for two decades in ministry, I've come to realize that, yes, there can be new models, many in fact.[9] The question is, Are there some principles that can guide us as we consider new forms of church that still reflect the Great Commandment and the Great Commission? I believe the answer is a resounding yes.

More than ever, our churches and ministries need to stand for something bigger than the prospects of our organizations and focus on summoning our people to live for something beyond themselves.

The church must tap into what's happening in society. Hardly a day goes by when we don't hear in the news of another example of how much the younger generation in America—and people of all ages throughout the world—cares about social justice, about living for the common good. They don't want just to make a living for themselves. They want to live for something much more fulfilling than self-interest.

Now, entire books could be devoted to explaining why and how this has happened. Part of the reason for this swing toward interest in social action, I believe, is that a savvy generation of young people has seen their parents relentlessly pursue and even realize dreams of wealth and achievement, but at painful, damaging cost to their relationships and health. The result: a very normal flame of adolescent rebellion fed by disillusionment with materialism and mainline institutions. And that flame has been fanned by communication technologies that make possible an unprecedented capacity for grassroots organization, coalition, and action among people worldwide.

This generation is ready to roll! And don't count out the suburban young people who are ripe for the third-culture movement of compassion because they have tasted the "American Dream" and are still hungry and increasingly disillusioned with what is defined as success.

At the same time, Boomers in America are entering the twilight of their lives, a season when people seek to make a lasting difference in the world they'll someday be leaving behind. And Boomers are better positioned than any prior generation to make that difference. They are the wealthiest generation ever, and they are living at a time when there are fewer barriers than ever to investing time and money in developing nations.

All of this presents an amazing opportunity for the church to become the most relevant, most vibrant, most vital element of people's lives—both to the young and the old. But to pull that off, we need to radically shift our thinking from believing that success means being a safe place for people to catch up and be together for an hour or two on Sunday and maybe hear an entertaining message, to recognizing that we are, first and foremost, a movement of people called to a dangerous mission.

If you look at the history of the church, this represents not so much a shift as a swing, a swing back to our roots. Historian Rodney Stark, in his great book, *The Rise of Christianity*, wonders why the Christian movement grew so rapidly in the first few centuries after Jesus' crucifixion. Its adherents were a small band of social outcasts. What transformed this ragtag group of zealots into a global movement at such a spectacular pace?

Stark's inquiry concluded that the surge in the growth of Christianity was rooted in the response of early Christians to a wave of great pandemics. At least two plagues wracked the developing world in the first three centuries after the death of Christ, and Christians did something no one else would do. They stayed. They helped. And many gave their lives in doing so.

In Stark's book, Dionysius, the bishop of Alexandria, described in a letter how believers responded to a deadly plague that killed an estimated five thousand people a day in the Roman Empire sometime around 260 AD: "Most of our brother Christians showed unbounded love and loyalty, never sparing themselves and thinking only of one another. Heedless of danger, they took charge of the sick, attending to their every need and ministering to them in Christ, and with them departed this life serenely happy; for they were infected by others with the disease, drawing on themselves the sickness of their neighbors and cheerfully accepting their pains. Many, in nursing and curing others, transferred their death to themselves and died in their stead.... The best of brothers lost their lives in this way."[10]

Such are our roots. Intuitively, we all know that this is what our churches are supposed to be about—caring for the weak and the poor, the distressed and the marginalized, the discouraged and the despairing. However, is our energy primarily directed toward creating a weekend church service? There's nothing wrong with doing excellent services on Sunday, but what about the other six days? I remember hearing about one church that has placards in their offices that read, "We live for Sundays." What does that say about the other six days? And another group says at their children's seminar, "We want the kids' Sunday morning to be the best hour of their week." Really? With or without the parents? Some fathers and mothers might disagree if they thought about it. Statements like these, while not totally off, do shed light on where our priorities are. They're a reflection of our values.

While events are important in the life of a community of believers, I wonder if we have drifted far from our central call to love God and love our neighbor. I'm sensing that the time has arrived for a significant shift, from consumerism to cause-ism. That's the first shift that marks a third-culture church.

### *From Pastor/Teacher to Pastor/Social Entrepreneur*

Here's a shift that goes to the heart of how a pastor views his role in this new world. I'll never forget when this shift first started to take on meaning for me. I was studying for ordination, and my required work had to do with comprehending God's heart for the impoverished. I always knew God wanted me as a pastor to care for the poor in some way, but I never realized to what degree.

To go through the ordination process, I read a lot of books about the intersection of church and poverty, listened to a lot of presentations, and even reviewed Scripture passages about the poor. In retrospect, I believe God was trying to show me something about myself and about being a pastor. But at the time, I kept shoving it out of mind. After all, I had a busy, growing church to focus on, a staff to develop, and a lengthy to-do list to whittle away at.

Well, while all of these thoughts were swirling in my mind, I stood before my staff in a meeting one day and a staff person walked in, interrupted us, shuffled up to me, and whispered, "Dave, we have a homeless woman living in our shed on the campus here. What do you want me to do?"

God was trying to get my attention. He was saying, "Dave, you cannot put this aside any longer, because this is your neighbor. Deal with this now."

My encounter with the homeless woman opened my eyes to aspects of this love God calls us to that had eluded me despite years in ministry. This woman gave me a priceless gift, a far richer understanding of what Jesus means when he says that our love for God and for others is what it's all about.

What does it mean for me? It means to be about loving unexpecting people, in unexpected ways, at unexpected times, to unexpected degrees.

It's being a father, a father whose actions, first, and words, second, reflect outrageous generosity and compassion—an advocacy for justice, a desire to be a blessing for a fatherless generation, and a source of unconditional love that embodies sacrifice, forgiveness, and servanthood. We must, first and foremost, occupy ourselves with and deal with the deepest needs within our hurting communities and society.

### *From Linear Pathways to Third-Culture Rhythms*

A well-known and respected church in Southern California recently rallied about ninety people to pull off a forty-eight-hour massive renovation of a broken-down, three-bedroom home for a family of twelve in Santa Ana, California. It was a wonderful act of kindness, and at the celebration held at the end of the job, many of those involved expressed how God had blessed them even more than the family whose home had been rebuilt.

One man, however, a lean, muscular, intense, bearded forty-something fellow who had kept to himself during most of the project, didn't say much. This guy had exhibited an amazing work ethic during the project. In fact, if you watched a videotape of the celebration, you'd see him hanging back in the crowd as they handed over the keys to the reconditioned house to the emotional family matriarch. You'd wonder if the man was truly enjoying himself and why he didn't seem to know anyone else.

There turned out to be a very good reason for all this. When one of the project leaders introduced himself to the man at the end to thank him for his help, he found out that the man didn't appear to know anyone from the church because he didn't go to the church. Or any church, for that matter. In fact, he confided in the project leader that he was pretty much an atheist. He'd read about the project in a small article in a local newspaper and simply thought it was a great idea and that his skills as a carpenter might prove helpful. So he just showed up. The guy apologized to the project leader and said he hoped it was okay that he'd joined the church construction crew, even if he was a bit covert about it.

The project leader found himself not only caught off-guard but also pondering the fact that, technically, the man should not have been allowed to help renovate this family's home. Why? Because the church, like many of our churches, requires people who do church work on behalf of its ministries in the community to be professing Christians. That had always made sense to the project leader, and he'd never given the requirement a second thought — until now.

The man expressed gratitude for the opportunity to pitch in and do a good deed, stabbed out his hand to say goodbye, politely smiled, and then told the project leader, "I can tell you this, though ... it's things like this that can make a guy start to believe in God."

This story illustrates a rhythms approach to ministry, life, and spiritual development that we at Newsong are embracing. For a long time now, churches have approached ministry and spiritual development as a linear progression. You accept Jesus as your Lord and Savior, and *then* you proceed down a well-defined path into the deeper truths of the faith. This systems approach has worked well in America and continues to have significant value, especially for segments of the Boomer age group and individuals who want structure and clear pathways.

But we have to understand and acknowledge that this Western, sequential, how-to approach has not resonated in much of the world. And it's not going to. This is especially true in the East, Africa, and Latin America, where God's Spirit is doing wonderful works these days. It also doesn't find a receptive audience with most people in post-Boomer generations in almost any country in the world, including in the West.

The linear approach works for solutions-oriented, efficiency-minded, and strategy-focused cultures and societies, such as twentieth-century America. But the ethos coming to life in our new world is requiring us to rethink how we approach and talk about spirituality and our relationship with God and his world. Some of the new forces at work include the democratization of the world; the flattening of authority structures in businesses and major social institutions; the appeal to grassroots values and methods in social problem-solving; the erosion of trust in leaders and institutions; the shifting of economic and cultural power and influence from West to East; and the movement from individualistic decision-making to tribal or corporate decision-making. (See table.)

| **Typical Western Pathways** | **Third-Culture Rhythms** |
|---|---|
| Linear | Adaptive/Liquid |
| Orderly Steps | Messy Journey |
| Individual | Community |
| Categorizes | Holistic |
| Teaches | Guides |
| Cookie-Cutter | Customized |
| Western | Eastern/Fusion |
| Comfort | Painful |
| Programmed | Artful |
| Homogeneous | Multicultural |

What makes sense to a broad swath of people I've encountered around the world and to younger people everywhere today is an ethic of spirituality that is far more messy. In fact, in the Newsong community we often talk about messiness. Generally speaking, the messier, the better.

Many people today are just like the man who came to the home-renovation project. They enter a relationship with Jesus through involvement in a cause or doing a good deed. They have no interest in "accepting Jesus as their Lord and Savior," but they want to be engaged in a worthwhile endeavor. That's likely to be their most effective introduction to Jesus and the gospel. So in today's culture, a person's religious conversion is better viewed as a dynamic, organic, messy journey—complete with detours and dead ends and back alleys and U-turns—than as a moment that triggers a series of key decisions.

The simple model of ministry that enfolds these principles is what we're calling the rhythms model. In this model, you organize ministry around three intersecting spheres—Christ, cause, and community. You need all three rhythms to be healthy. A person can be operating within one sphere, two spheres, or all three; any of those scenarios leads a person closer to Jesus, no matter where they are spiritually, as the story about the man in the remodeling project illustrates.

This approach really makes sense in the global culture taking shape today, and because it's more consistent with how people make decisions and live their lives, it seems to have more traction with the next generation, which insists on the convergence of both the realities and the mysteries of life. Using this approach, we're finding that people are more open to pursuing the one who embodies transcendence, reality, and mystery, which, at the end of the day, is what Christian spiritual growth is about—a lifelong journey of loving and living as Jesus did.

# Three Questions That Become the Answers

I refuse to accept the view that mankind is so tragically bound to the starless midnight of racism and war that the bright daybreak of peace and brotherhood can never become a reality.... I believe that unarmed truth and unconditional love will have the final word.

—Martin Luther King Jr.

Freedom is not worth having if it does not connote freedom to err. It passes my comprehension how human beings, be they ever so experienced and able, can delight in depriving other human beings of that precious right.

—Mahatma Gandhi

I wonder if the lyrics to this song will be familiar to some of you.

> Life was filled with guns and war
> And everyone got trampled on the floor.
> I wish we'd all been ready.

Children died, the days grew cold,
A piece of bread could buy a bag of gold.
I wish we'd all been ready.

—Larry Norman,
"I Wish We'd All Been Ready"

The song goes on to repeat in a depressing tone how there isn't any time to change your mind because Jesus has come and there is no doubt, you've been left behind! That song about the rapture, the second coming of Jesus, scared the living daylights out of me when I was in elementary school. I had nightmares of being left behind.

I still vividly remember coming home from school and the house was eerily quiet. With a trembling voice, I cried out, "Mom? Dad? Doug?" Doug is my brother. Out of the darkness came this voice. It was Doug. I was ecstatic at first but then realized, man, he was on the fence; he was undecided! He could be left behind too!

You don't know how sweet it was when I finally heard one of my parents' voice. The rapture hadn't happened yet! Whew.

Now, that was a terrifying experience for me, but equally, if not more, horrifying is the church's missing out on God's plans for this global village. We don't want to miss out on the miracles that are unfolding and will unfold in our lifetime as we live out his third-culture mandate.

### Shift Happens

You may have seen the YouTube video "Shift Happens." If not, go to youtube.com and type in "shift happens."

Check out the text and message of the video. It'll rock your world.

Basically, the video powerfully communicates the massive shifts that have happened globally. One example of the dramatic impact of this video presentation is when they say,

> During the course of this 8 minute presentation ...
>
> 60 babies will be born in the U.S.
>
> 244 babies will be born in China.
>
> 351 babies will be born in India.

Throughout the video, the effect of the rise of China and India on American jobs, education, wealth, standards of living, and military position is evident. Moreover, in the information era, our technological infrastructures and public initiatives seem to be lagging behind Asia's. Yes, the writers of this video effectively get their point across: shift happens. We're living in the middle of a transition that will mark the way we do church for the next century. With information and answers in flux, with new technologies that spread knowledge more quickly than ever dreamed, an unsettling tremor is shaking the religious world.

Those of us who don't like change probably will be tempted to resort to being hermits to protect ourselves from such change. Hence, we'll sit out on possibly one of the greatest spiritual shifts in history.

But for those brave, crazy people among us who love dissonant sounds and multidirectional winds, this is the moment we've been waiting for. It's the wave of possibility we've dreamed about.

So what are we supposed to do? How do we navigate the currents of change? How do we do church in this chaotic environment? What strategies and approaches should we create and pursue? How do we become the church that isn't left behind, that can both last and make a lasting difference? What are some things we can start doing today?

Well, I've found it's not so much about the answers as it is about the questions. Questions will lead us.

## Questions, Instead of Answers, Will Guide Us

Not long ago I was privileged to participate in a series of gatherings over a two-year period to learn from a variety of respected business and Christian gurus. One of the sessions featured Max DePree, the nationally known, bestselling author and former CEO of the Herman Miller Company. DePree once received from the president of the United States one of the highest awards a civilian can get for his achievements as a business person.

In the audience, we were primed and ready to glean DePree's wisdom. As he took the podium, we gave him our rapt attention. And yet his very first words greatly disappointed me.

"Today we're going to talk about one of the most important aspects of leadership. We're going to talk about questions, rather than answers. We're going to spend our time together today talking about the great questions of life. What are they? When it comes to our church? Our personal lives? Our ministries? Let's not talk about what some of the answers might be; let's talk about the questions."

I was taken aback and started having this little dialogue in my mind. "But wait a second, I came to hear *you.* I want my fixes, my portfolio of solutions to take back to my constituents. I want to know how to organize my life. I want to know how to do church and ministry better. I don't want to waste time asking questions."

I've come to realize how wise this process is. Max knew that the answer finds its residence in the question. While an answer may work in a specific circumstance, questions can guide us to the answers in all kinds of situations.

Just ask any teacher. Most teachers will tell you that a lesson filled with thought-provoking questions takes more time to develop than one in which you download information to your students through a thirty-minute lecture.

People frequently ask me how I come up with strategic methods, programs, and approaches to use in a given context, whether that's a suburb in America, a rural town in Pennsylvania, a world-class urban environment like Seoul or Los Angeles, or a village in Southeast Asia. My response is that while the answers are different for each context, I have a grid of questions that guides me.

## Lights That Guide Us Home

Three questions have guided me in ministry, in other organizations I've started and been a part of, and in my personal life. These questions can point you in a direction that is tailored to how God has made you and to how you and your organization can make a difference in the world.

### *1. Where Is Nazareth?*

"Can anything good come from Nazareth?" This question was asked about Jesus. Can anyone worthwhile come from that place on the other side of the railroad tracks?

Where is the other side of tracks in your city or region? In other words, who are the marginalized or the outsiders near you, people whom you feel pain for?

This question about Nazareth focuses us because it's contrary to the church-growth mentality of focusing only on people just like us. It's built on the premise, as we discussed earlier, that our neighbors are people who are different from us.

Newsong was birthed as a response to this question. I became concerned about ethnic groups that were misfits in many American churches and denominations, churches that were reaching a white, suburban, middle-class, technology-savvy demographic based on church-growth oriented, seeker-sensitive ideology. Again, church growth, or health by numbers, should not be our driving factor, because we can be big and yet unhealthy, and we can look healthy but be creating a church that doesn't reflect the mandate of the second most important commandment, to love our neighbors. We can wind up with just a church of a lot of people like us, a church where Christians basically just change their local church zip codes.

As we continued asking this question at Newsong, it led us to start a church in what is considered to be one of the murder capitals of America: Crenshaw, California. We started a multisite church in the Los Angeles area not to franchise our church but to love people who need love without strings—gangs, the homeless, single moms. Crenshaw became our goal because we asked ourselves, Who are the marginalized, the misfits, in our region?

When we launched a Newsong site in Bangkok, the same question guided us. We saw thousands of neglected children in the slums hidden behind the glitz and power of a skyline gleaming with corporate towers. As we meditated on this question, we were led to meet and help three groups: the struggling but influential artists' community in Bangkok; the Issan people, the most marginalized people group in Thailand, who are trying to eke out some type of life in Bangkok; and the sad, huge community of prostitutes working in a country whose gross national product is disproportionately fed by the sex industry.

We've gone through a similar process as we've started churches and ministries in the United Kingdom, Mexico City, and India.

So who in your community is the outsider, the misjudged, the misunderstood? Maybe the one who seems the weakest? Who are the strangers and friendless? Focusing on them as a church may mean you won't grow as fast. And you may lose some people. But your church will be fulfilling the most beautiful expression of who God is.

Paul said it perfectly in his letter to the church in Corinth—God uses the weak of the world to confound the mighty and accomplish God's biggest dreams. "Remember, dear brothers and sisters, that few of you were wise in the world's eyes, or powerful, or wealthy when God called you. Instead, God deliberately chose things the world considers foolish in order to shame those who think they are wise. And he chose those who are powerless to shame those who are powerful. God chose things despised by the world, things counted as nothing at all, and used them to bring to nothing what the world considers important, so that no one can ever boast in the presence of God" (1 Cor. 1:26–29 NLT).

### *2. What Is My Pain?*

I come from the generation that used personality tests, spiritual gifts inventories and analyses, SHAPE tests, and whatever else could equip our people to make a difference.

Having business interests, I loved the tests and have used them frequently to turn our spectators into participants. But when's the last time we've meditated on who God uses and what God uses in their lives?

I'm discovering that most people can't relate to our achievements or successes. However, most people can relate to our pain and our losses, our disappointments and our suffering.

It seems as if our Western-style of pop Christianity has drifted toward a prosperity-blessing motif. *Five Ways to Having the Greatest Life on the Planet* type books are pretty popular, it seems. Easter is the biggest day of the year, and it should be.

However, I think South American and Eastern countries can help us with our theology and lifestyle. They not only think of resurrection day but also have a theology of suffering and pain. It's not just about the resurrection; it's about the Via Dolorosa—the way of suffering. It's about the journey of pain to the cross.

What will draw most of the world to Christ is not simply a prosperity gospel but a gospel that takes a real look at the beauty and the bane of suffering. The apostle Paul says in his letter to the Corinthians, "I will destroy human wisdom and discard their most brilliant ideas." He goes on, "So where does this leave the philosophers, the scholars, and the world's brilliant debaters? God has made them all look foolish and has shown their wisdom to be useless nonsense. Since God in his wisdom saw to it that the world would never find him through human wisdom, he has used our foolish preaching to save all who believe. God's way seems foolish to the Jews because they want a sign from heaven to prove it is true. And it is foolish to the Greeks because they believe only what agrees with their own wisdom. So when we preach that Christ was crucified, the Jews are offended, and the Gentiles say it's all nonsense" (1 Cor. 1:19–23 NLT).

The core of the gospel message isn't prosperity but foolishness! The message was Christ crucified. The Jews couldn't understand this because they were expecting a messiah who would come with power and bring prosperity.

The Scriptures are filled with passages that reflect this idea. In Isaiah 6, Isaiah is captivated by the greatness of God, ready to go anywhere and do anything, but few pastors preach about what happens after Isaiah declares, "Lord, I'll go! Send me." God says to Isaiah, "Yes, go. But tell my people this: 'You will hear my words, but you will not understand. You will see what I do, but you will not perceive its meaning.' Harden the hearts of these people. Close their ears, and shut their eyes. That way, they will not see with their eyes, hear with their ears, understand with their hearts, and turn to me for healing."

I love Isaiah's response: "Lord, how long must I do this?"

Can you feel Isaiah's pain as he realizes he's in over his head?

And God replies, "Until their cities are destroyed, with no one left in them. Until their houses are deserted and the whole country is an utter wasteland. Do not stop until the LORD has sent everyone away to distant lands and the entire land of Israel lies deserted. Even if only a tenth—a remnant—survive, it will be invaded again and burned. Israel will remain a stump, like a tree that is cut down, but the stump will be a holy seed that will grow again" (NLT).

Pain, you see, was going to allow Israel to become the holy seed. But first they would be a stump.

Personally, as I've periodically inventoried my life, I've listed all the painful moments, the moments of sadness and suffering involving the people in my life. My parents' divorce. My mom's death at the hands of a drunken driver. My being told in college at a Christian university that I couldn't see my girlfriend because I was Asian-American and she was Caucasian. Friends who've left me feeling betrayed or disillusioned. And I've realized again and again that my pain was a gift from God. As I've met people around the world and shared my pain with them, it is the pain that draws people in, far more so than my limited talents, skills, and accomplishments. It disarms all the things that can be used to divide us—race, economics, culture, politics, nationalism, dogma, language.

This is why I love stories of people like Rahab. She was a prostitute, despised and hated by women and abused by men. Yet God would redeem her pain and lift her up as a heroine of the faith in Hebrews 11.

And not only that, God could have chosen to be born among the rulers and powerbrokers of the day, but instead God chose to have Jesus be born on the other side of the tracks in a place like Nazareth and decided he'd have great-grandmothers like Bathsheba, an adulteress, and, you guessed it, Rahab. Why? I think it's because most of the world can relate better and more positively to a prostitute who humbly admits her shortcomings than to some of us who have learned to manage our image and pimp the gospel. One is not hiding her identity and is at least honest about what she's selling. The other is often selling something too but is less honest and humble about it and dares to do so in the name of God.

It's worth reminding ourselves that Jesus didn't come from a line of professional clergy and had no social pedigree. He came from real, flawed people who weren't necessarily proud of their past and didn't like their pain, but he embraced them and, by faith, saw something far better come of them.

### *3. What Is in My Hand?*

This is another way of asking, What has God already given me? Instead of wishing for and complaining about what I don't have, what do I have today? Instead of dangerously comparing myself with others, what is within my grasp relationally, historically, and resources-wise right now?

There's a powerful lesson for us in the famous account in the book of Exodus of Moses' encounter with God. Whenever I read of Moses' assignment from God to oversee the liberation of the Israelites from Egypt and lead them to the Promised Land, I can tell that Moses wasn't feeling it! He was probably thinking about the good old days of solitude and shepherding, and he wasn't at all enchanted with the assignment of leading tens of thousands of people out of Egypt.

Now, Moses is a lot more like us than we imagine, and you can see this in his response to God's action plan. Just as we often do, he quickly comes up with reasons why God's plan probably won't work. And actually Moses chirps out a pretty decent excuse when he says in Exodus 4:1–5 (NLT):

> "Look, they won't believe me! They'll just say, 'The LORD never appeared to you.' "
>
> Then the LORD asked him, "What do you have there in your hand?"
>
> "A shepherd's staff," Moses replied.
>
> "Throw it down on the ground," the LORD told him. So Moses threw it down, and it became a snake! Moses was terrified, so he turned and ran away.
>
> Then the LORD told him, "Take hold of its tail." So Moses reached out and grabbed it, and it became a shepherd's staff again.
>
> "Perform this sign, and they will believe you," the LORD told him. "Then they will realize that the LORD, the God of their ancestors—the God of Abraham, the God of Isaac, and the God of Jacob—really has appeared to you."

Hmm. It would seem that Moses, like us, is focused more on what he doesn't have than on what he actually has. God promises he will be with him, but Moses is afraid that the people won't follow him.

Moses looks at himself and seriously doubts that he has what it takes.

It does seem as if the leadership path is a rewind of constant self-doubt and paralysis, doesn't it? Any worthy endeavor is constrained by our worst fears. For Moses, one of his demons is losing the respect of the people he is called to lead. But as he starts to tremble at the thought of potential humiliation from a potential failure of leadership, God asks him, "What is in your hand?"

Everything we need is within our reach and within his reach.

In ministry, I've seen how easy it is for us to focus on what we lack:

Money
The right staff
Encouraging supporters
Mentors
Education
Buildings
Healthy family history
The right experience
Communication skills
Knowledge

The list could go on ad infinitum.

I've learned that our focus too often drifts toward what we don't have, and we overlook what is already in our hand.

It may look like a simple stick—an old, twisted, knobby piece of wood—but God can turn it into something that can bring both fear and hope into peoples' eyes and remind them of his supernatural ability and constant presence.

Maybe the most significant thing God placed in my hand is something I saw for a long time as a curse.

As a kid, I was always embarrassed about being Asian. In my youth in Arizona, I was one of about five Asians in a school of more than two thousand students. My goal was always just to blend in.

My father was Caucasian with blue eyes. My mom was a feisty, five-foot-tall Korean. I guess, like it is with many children of immigrants, I was horribly embarrassed by my mom. When we went to the mall, she walked into a department store and tried to get them to lower the prices! If we went out to eat, she sneaked up to the all-you-can-eat buffet lines and took extra chicken back to her seat. She pulled out a napkin and wrapped up the fried chicken and stuffed it into her purse! In high school, I seriously thought I'd die of embarrassment.

Only after my mom died did I come to realize what I was given through her life and through my parents' multiracial marriage. I'd been given a gift! It was the gift of being third culture, the gift of being more appreciative and in love with the beauty and wisdom that different cultures can gain from one another. What I once saw as a terrible, even embarass-ing, burden was in fact a transformational blessing. As I've examined my life and ministry and prayed about the future, it's this multicultural family history that has pointed me to the whole notion of doing third-culture, global work.

God takes what we have in our hand and turns it into something powerful to show us and the world that he is there and is working and is with us. Even my parents' divorce, our house burning down when I was in third grade, our cross-country move, my ethnic roots—all were part of a compass that guided me home.

So what is in *your* hand?

As you look at the misfits and outsiders of your community, you don't have to focus only on soup-kitchen ministries. God may have you create artists' communities, cafes, urban lounges, tutoring centers, English language schools, marine biology research centers, fish farms, music labs, music labels, T-shirt design companies, venture capital companies, strategic boards, technology centers—all of these have been created at one time or another by people in our Newsong community; people who have come to realize that God will take the talent, the knowledge, and the resources within our reach and turn them into something that others will say is "Made by God"; people who have seen firsthand how these three questions about Nazareth, our pain, and what's in our hand can guide us through the tumult and tension, the triumphs and thrills of serving God as best we can. They are questions that have guided me. And my prayer, and my conviction, is they will do the same for you.

# cWoWs

## Everyone Plays

> Your task is not to seek for love, but merely to seek and find all the barriers within yourself that you have built against it.
>
> —Jalal ad-Din Rumi

> I think where we need to look now is to the same source that the people of the twelfth and thirteenth centuries did when their civilization was foundering: to the poets and artists. These people can look past the broken symbols of the present and begin to forge new working images, images that are transparent to transcendent.
>
> —Joseph Campbell

Martin Luther personified boldness. His life was filled with passion and a sense of urgency for the church to be what she was destined to be. Bottlenecks and barriers and abuse of power and position were his targets.

His early years were marked by prayer, fasting, and confession. He later remarked, "If anyone could have gained heaven as a monk, then I would indeed have been among them."

His boldness grew out of a fire burning within him. He challenged the authority of the papacy, maintaining that the Scriptures are the sole source of religious authority.

He also proclaimed the priesthood of all believers. Later, Luther translated the Bible into the German vernacular, making the Bible available for the first time to common people.

What Luther is most often remembered for is his posting of what came to be known as the Ninety-five Theses. He vehemently opposed the church's practice of selling indulgences. In Roman Catholic theology, an indulgence was the remission of punishment because a sin already committed had been forgiven. The indulgence was granted by the church once the sinner confessed and received absolution. When an indulgence was given, the church was extending merit to a sinner from its treasure house of merit, an accumulation of merits the church had collected based on the good deeds of the saints. At the time, these merits could be bought and sold. Eventually, by decree of Pope Pius V in 1567, following the Council of Trent, it was forbidden to attach the receipt of an indulgence to any financial act.

Luther loved the church, and he believed it was long past time to remove her bottlenecks and barriers.

### The Big Squeeze

We ask this question a lot among the community of believers I do life with: What are the bottlenecks of our church?

What are the barriers? What squeezes the life out of what is intended to be a sanctuary of strength and a source of life, hope, and intimacy?

We also have wondered the same about the church at large.

And one of the biggest issues we've come to recognize is similar to what Luther found—there's a structure, organization, and philosophy that discourages and hinders, if not prevents, the involvement and collaboration of everyday people in the most important parts of church and ministry.

Too often it seems like church ends up being all about place and not nearly enough about people.

Too often it seems like preconceived notions about the form of the church trump the reason for the church's existance in the first place.

We're seeing that every time we make church not about a place or form but instead a home where *everyone* plays—a church without walls—we end up with something liberating, empowering, and engaging.

What's adding urgency to being a church without walls is that all around the world we're seeing a dramatic flattening of hierarchies and loosening of structures in significant domains and institutions, and moves toward decentralization that are common during seasons of innovation.

Because of the internet and peer-to-peer platforms like Wikipedia, YouTube, Facebook, MySpace, and others, ordinary people around the world are participating and collaborating in ways and in spaces they never did before. And they are demonstrating there's vast expertise and talent out there that just didn't have a voice or vehicle before. A new collaboration in the world is eradicating fences and removing age-old barriers, bullies, budgets, biases, and bottlenecks.

But what about in the church?

## Fiesta Bowl Champions!

Okay, hold your applause, but I was once a part of a football team that won the Fiesta Bowl in Arizona.

I still remember crouching in my three-point stance ready to block the guy in front of me. I was sweating. I felt the energy of the crowd and the coaches watching my every move. But before I knew it, the game was over.

Well, at least it was for me. Maybe that was because I played only one whole minute, a minute that was inconsequential to the outcome of the game. We had the game locked up when I finally got picked to go in. All the guys on my team were nine or ten years old. We were in a league of NFL wannabes called Pop Warner Football. Some of the guys on that team actually became pretty good football players that I later played against in high school.

Sure, I still have the red, white, and blue trophy for the Fiesta Bowl victory. It has a proud position on my shelf in the garage above the stately washing machine!

So why don't I appreciate the trophy all that much?

Well, I really wasn't integral to the team. I was on the roster, yes. I was given a token role in an inconsequential series of plays, yes. But I was someone the coaches had to play because his parents had forked over some good cash and were wondering when their son was going to get on the field.

It wasn't a great experience. I still remember my dad saying to me in a game one time, "Why don't they play you? I come to your games. I'm just wasting my time."

Now, even though I'm not bitter and am not possessed by a need to somehow prove those old coaches of mine wrong, the truth is that that memory is a vivid one for me.

It also reminds me of churches and religious organizations.

How often do people in church feel that they are able to be involved in meaningful ministry activities?

Doesn't it seem like the best work, or the most "spiritual" work, is reserved for the pastors?

How often do those in the congregational team actually feel like they are on the front lines, passionately pursuing their dreams and aspirations?

I wonder if most don't feel like the third-string team that plays only if the game is well in hand.

## Church without Walls

Let me tell you about a pretty unusual scene. Had you walked into the ultrahip nightclub district in downtown Bangkok called the Royal City Avenue (RCA) on a Sunday evening not long ago, you would have noticed something pretty strange. Sunday's a day when hundreds of young people, mostly in their twenties, cram into Slim, one of the trendiest clubs in all of Thailand, while most RCA visitors are at home nursing hangovers or recounting the hazy details of the prior night's one-night stands.

In a spot where young tourists and partiers from around the globe were bumping and grinding just twelve hours earlier, this international group of young people is listening to a guy who looks like an MTV VJ talking to them about dehydration. He's explaining—in whimsical terms—how drinking too much drains all the liquid from a person's brain and that's why you end up with a killer headache the day after a night of heavy boozing. And that, he tells them, is why drinking lots of water is the number one key to preventing or treating a hangover.

Then the speaker explains how in life we can become dehydrated in much more profound ways. It doesn't matter if you're American, European, African, or Asian, we all want to be significant. We all want to know that we matter. And we all try lots of ways to deal with this spiritual dehydration. We pursue all sorts of things in life—wealth, sex, drugs, power, fame, materialism, recognition, accomplishment—to stop the pain of this killer spiritual hangover.

And just as water is about the only cure for the pain of a hangover, he goes on, there's a kind of water that can help heal the pains we go through in this life. It's a water that will quench our deepest thirst. You can't have a life without pain, he tells them. That's part of being human. But it's how you respond to your pain and misfortune and disappointment that matters most. There's a path not only to help you understand your pain and grow from it but also to help you live a life that will be a blessing to you, the people you love, and God.

Now, before I tell you how this particular evening ended, let's consider the crazy unlikelihood of this scene. It's taking place in Thailand, a country where more than 95 percent of the people are Buddhists and where 60 percent of the unstated gross domestic product comes from the sex industry. It's taking place in a region of Bangkok advertised worldwide on the internet as the destination spot for young pleasure-seekers.

Yes, it's a pretty unlikely place for church, but that's exactly what it is.

## A Party in Bangkok!

We ended up in the RCA district of Bangkok for our gatherings because we figured that was the place in Bangkok with the fewest barriers to attracting the kind of people we really wanted to love on. We also wanted it to be fun, to be a playground, a place where young people would love to come back and bring their friends, and a place where anyone can be involved, including in the most significant parts of the gathering, such as sharing or singing.

Listen to how one of our many volunteers describes how it works:

"Well, a lot of the process is very fluid. Things happen spontaneously. People are free to share ideas, and the people tend to have ideas that come from a heart that shares the core values. That is, we need to have a place where people are known, where people feel valued, where people know each others' names, and where everybody can be involved. We need a place where people can be connected to God and reconciled to Jesus. We need a place where people can reach out and meet needs and be part of a greater picture and have influence in the world around them.

"Sometimes there is a plan. But a lot of times there is this amazing connection that happens and someone says, 'Well, who's going to speak and who's going to share?' And someone will say, 'God has been telling me this.' And, 'Oh! That's perfect and you can share and you can do that.'

"And then someone will say, 'Well, I was writing this song this week.' And it's, 'Oh, will you sing that song this week?'

"There are things that have to be planned, and we plan it ahead and we think of budgets and we think of speakers and who is going to be here and when. We do things like that. But a lot of times, things happen and it is as if God is up there looking at the angels and saying, 'Okay, wait a minute, wait, wait, wait . . . there!' And a connection happens or somebody meets somebody else, and these spontaneous, divine moments happen that, to a type-A personality, would look like chaos. But embracing chaos is not such a bad thing."

No, it's not. And while it naturally has its challenges, it often can have some pretty good outcomes too. At the close of this particular Slim gathering, many young Thais and others visiting from other countries raised their hands to say that they wanted to know more about this person called Jesus. It was an amazing moment.

Since we started that gathering in Bangkok, our Newsong community has supported our going and doing likewise in other places as varied as Mexico City, Los Angeles' Skid Row, and London. In each place, what the church gathering looks like may be different, but it is consistently derived from the question, What does it look like here, wherever here is, to have a place without walls and where everybody plays?

## Pubs in London

What's working really well in London, a place where the church has been declared dead and gone for a long time, especially for young people, is a three-pronged approach. Here again, it's better coming from one of our leaders, Dave Brubaker, than from me.

"In London we've got Pub Nights, we've got the Underground, and then we've got the Sunday night dinners at our house. The leadership development part is the Underground. That's where the leaders get together and it's very informal.

"The Pub Night is like the party that everyone is invited to. The thing that I would say most resembles heaven in London, the time where I just step back and go, 'This is the kingdom, this is what it is supposed to look like, this is "on earth as it is in heaven," my dream come true,' is Sunday nights at our house.

"Basically, it started as a few international students who said, 'Hey, let's do English class and look at the Bible together.' It has become this massive feast that has people from everywhere in the world who live in London coming over every Sunday, and there's almost always six or seven different languages being spoken!

"The Sunday-night dinners started when I first got to London and was still trying to figure out what to do. I was at the library and I saw a couple of girls who had just moved to London from Korea and they were studying English. We were going to have a barbeque for Easter and I was just feeling that I should invite them. So I had this little ghetto flyer that I printed off on my computer, it was the lamest thing ever, and I went over and said, 'Hey, me and my wife and our friends are from America. If you want to come over and speak English with us . . .' I swear it was that lame. But it was instantly that they said, 'Yes, we will be there.'

"We don't do Bible studies per se, because we look at ourselves as learning together with them. It's, 'Where do I see God's fingerprints on this person? Where do I see God's fingerprints on this group of people?' It's me saying to this young Korean girl, 'I have watched you and every time that I see you and as we have been hanging out the last few months, you totally remind me of this verse in the Bible. And I just want to thank you because you are teaching me about this verse.' It's not me saying, 'You should be living this way or that way.' It's, 'You remind me of this and I just want to say thank *you* for teaching *me* what that verse looks like to be lived out.' Again, it is the craziest thing. People, when they come on Sundays, they have wandered into the kingdom and they don't even know it.

"Now non-church people are the ones who are inviting their friends to our house every Sunday. And there are another five or six new people every single week, and the non-Christian is the one who is telling their other non-Christian friends, 'Dude, I don't care what you believe, you have to be here on Sunday. You are not going to believe this!'

"The Pub Nights are basically based on what Rob Bell said in that amazing book *Velvet Elvis*, where he said, 'We don't have much to say to the world until we can throw a better party.' Otherwise, what are we really inviting people to? If the party they're going to in the world is more fun, and they are laughing more, and they feel more accepted, and more at peace and more fulfilled at the end of the night, if we don't have that same joy, what do we have to offer? Our party should be the best.

"And in London, it is. Our Pub Nights have sold out everywhere we've gone. That is why the venues want *us*. There are different venues arguing over us, 'No, come to us! We will offer you this: our capacity is five hundred and we will give you three private rooms and we will guarantee you the first Saturday of the month'!

"Our guys send out a couple hundred texts and we get a few hundred people every time easily. We have outgrown every venue that we have been in. There's this guy who opened the Barfly, which is one of the most well-known pubs in London, one of the best live-music venues. Well, he is opening a new line of pubs and the first thing he wants is to book our Pub Night; he wants to host it!"

## Skid Row in Los Angeles

Another one of our churches without walls takes place every Friday night at the corner of Wall and Winston streets in the Skid Row section of downtown Los Angeles. The area gets talked about regularly in the news media as being one of the most drug-infested areas in the United States. Even as teenage "scramblers" ride by on their bikes shouting, "One time rolling!"—a warning to the crack-cocaine dealers that a police car is approaching—a mosaic of nationalities shows up and gathers in a circle for prayer and conversation and for handouts of food and water. One of the people who shows up regularly to give out the food is one of the most well-known

Asian chefs in Southern California. It's truly a place where the walls of the church, in every way, are about as high as they can be, but the almost-all-volunteer ministry team is out doing their best to knock them down.

Stephen "Cue" Jean-Marie is the chief wall crusher at the place known as the Row. "What happens with church without walls," he says, "is it frees up something that is laying dormant in that place, in that culture. It's kind of like when Jesus said, 'I want to do some miracles here, but I can't because of your unbelief.' I believe that when we do the church-without-walls thing, what happens is the love of God is like a virus that's been laying dormant in that particular context, and it finally gets airborne. No matter where you are, when *people* are the church, that love can become viral."

### The New ABCs

I love education and seminary. I've logged twenty-one years of formal training myself. But our ideas about who's qualified to lead in our churches and ministries and how they can participate have created a barrier for us in today's culture.

It's a new day. Look closely and you will notice a powerful trend—the emergence of a growing network of innovators and influencers operating in the world who are artists, businesspersons, and community-development specialists.

In every generation, it seems, God highlights different gifts and occupations to connect deeper with the world. Together, artists, businesspersons, and community-development specialists are today leading local transformations all around the world.

Not only do church and ministry in the twenty-first century need to be about people, and not a place, and to be a playground where everyone plays, but it's also essential that artists, businesspersons, and community-development specialists get some real focus.

Why these three disciplines and why now?

Well, acting without the constraints and limitations of institutions and governments and aided by technology, people in these three disciplines, helped by doctors, sports stars, and educators, have managed to design creative solutions to all kinds of social ills in so many places—gang violence in Connecticut, economic inequities in South Africa, warring tribes in Mali, gun violence in Brazil, religious conflict in Northern Ireland, drug victims in Colombia, and the list goes on.

Artists have moved to the center of the world's stage, using their standing and platforms for social good. They've come to be respected by tens of millions, both ordinary citizens and those occupying the seats of power, for their creativity and an ability to connect with widely diverse cultures. They create the language, metaphors, and images to communicate ideas and values. Artists play a prophetic role in movements.

Businesspersons bring capital, know how, and access as the fortunes of nations have become so closely interconnected through increased trade and commerce. This is the sector that can help create sustainability for communities and provide front-line wisdom to organizations and systems. They are the first to respond to emergencies. I remember a lecture by Peter

Drucker in which he said something like, "What business leaders need is the ethics of the church, and what the church needs is systems from corporations." He is right. Every corporation of any kind needs organization, the church more than any other. We also need entrepreneurs and risk-takers who are willing to help fuel new endeavors to see communities really changed.

Community-development specialists possess the view from the streets and the passion for change no matter where they are in the world. These are educators, health professionals, social-justice lawyers, spiritual support teams, relief workers, and economic developers.

Artists, businesspersons, and community-development specialists are in every church of any size. I think they can make a phenomenal difference in our churches and in our communities, especially in the eyes of seekers and skeptics. They have already emerged as a new wave of spiritual prophets, priests, and pioneers—at least in the eyes of much of the world.

We need to do all we can to identify them, team them up with one another, equip them, and unleash them.

This will require a sizable shift in our thinking and methods. Just as we struggle with biases about the kind of place church needs to be in, many of our churches struggle with systems that inhibit leaders and change agents. It's too often that people with God-given talents and skills see themselves only as financial givers and ancillary workers in the church.

The church is the largest social network in the world, but it's also one of the few organizations locally and globally that doesn't collaborate well. I was in New York City recently speaking to one of the top fund managers in the world. He was surprised to discover how infrequently churches collaborate, and how we just don't excel at collaboration at virtually any level. Even people we consider to be pagan often are much better at working together than the church is. I'm afraid our obsolete systems and hierarchies and thinking are making the church far more insular than we imagine.

A conversation with one of the most talented and well-known music composers in the Far East underscored this again for me recently. His name is Boyd Kosiyabang, and he's a Christ-follower. I asked him why he hasn't written any worship songs. He has millions of fans and admirers and could have a great impact in helping to create a new generation of worship songs for young people in the East. But he told me, "There are just too many rules."

I asked him who had told him that and he said, "That's what I learned from the church."

"Look," I told him, "there are no rules. Why don't you just write what you feel God wants you to write?"

He said, "Really?"

I don't think I said anything many of you wouldn't have said in the same circumstance, but it was as if shackles had fallen off the hands of this gifted young man.

Again, we need to empower our people to be deeply engaged in the exciting stuff we're doing, not just the supporting work we feel comfortable with them doing.

Max DePree, former CEO of Herman Miller, shared with a group I got to be a part of that for a church to be its best, it has to involve its people in the "best" work. In the case of artists, businesspersons, and community-development specialists, we need to help them understand how their gifting, skills, and passion can be of unprecedented service to God's activity in the world today. They don't have to become professional missionaries or pastors to live a fulfilling, adventurous life for God and do sacred, meaningful work. They are already an empowered priesthood.

## The Blurring of the Lines

Way back in 1809, a Cherokee Indian named Sequoyah learned to sign his name on his silversmith work. That was his introduction to the written language. A few years later, he fought with the US Army during the Creek War, and he observed American soldiers writing letters, reading orders, and recording historical events of the war. Sequoyah realized that the Cherokee nation could benefit immensely from a written language. Sequoyah worked on a written language for the Cherokee people for more than a decade. The language was so easy to learn that within weeks thousands of Cherokee were reading, and it gave the Cherokee nation the ability to create the first Native American newspaper, *The Cherokee Phoenix*. Sequoyah is the only person in the world known to have created an entire written language on his own, and he is regarded as a genius to this day.

What's beautiful about this account is how Sequoyah got the idea for creating a language after spending meaningful time in a culture other than his own. That's one of the benefits of loving the neighbor who is so different from you!

In addition to being critical to creating new stories and language, artists help bridge cultural and socio-economic differences. They can help bring down cultural barriers and create unity among diversity.

Sometimes I wonder what an artist like Shakira would say to the church.

Shakira is an icon for the new type of multicultural-loving influencer-leader in the arts. She rocked the US music scene with her groundbreaking album, *Laundry Service*. This Latin-American artist has a unique style of music even for her own country of Colombia. Her father is Lebanese, and her music started out as a fusion of Latin and Arabic sounds. Then she took her blend of music and converged it with American sounds. Her music combines Alanis Morissette, reggae, and Mexican mariachi bands.

*Newsweek* magazine wrote about her cross-cultural appeal, "Young stars like ... the Colombian rocker Shakira break down the division by mixing a variety of pop styles, Latin and Anglo. 'We are made of fusion,' Shakira says. 'It's what determines our identity.'"

Really, she's speaking for an entire generation around the world.

### Artists: Prophets, Innovators, and Conversationalists

Like Shakira and Sequoyah, artists are the creators of new ideas and forms of communication. They are the prophets of every generation. Artists help to codify ideas.

In the past, artists in the church were considered side attractions to the main element, the Sunday message. They were considered good preludes or complements to the spoken word. Now they are the message. They're modern-day prophets with pens, paintbrushes, and poetry.

Music and the arts are the language of each generation. They can incite revolution. They're the emotion and color that spark and sustain movements.

### Businesspersons: Access, Networks, Fuel

This should be a new day for businesspersons in the church, because for too long they have felt like second-class citizens there. Businessmen have come up to me sharing how they are leading multi-million-dollar companies with hundreds and thousands of employees but the church's leadership struggles to see them as more than simply human ATMs.

Businesspersons are the fuel for our movement. They can help lead entrepreneurial initiatives that spark the church's initiatives locally and globally. They often have the mix of creativity, sustainable management skills, and systems knowledge that keep any organization on mission.

The more a business leader can work in the intersections of culture, the more likely she or he will be successful in the new world order. They have to gravitate to the blur—and so do we.

In New York City there is a store named Kimera, after the Greek monster that is a combination of a lion, a goat, and a snake. This store features clothes with a blend of cultures. For example, one shirt may have both a kimono and a Western style to it. Yvonne Chu, the founder, says she draws much of her inspiration from her roots, her Chinese parents, who lived in New York, as well as her travels. She says people love the mixture of cultures in her clothing. She adds, "This shirt—people just went crazy for it." What type of shirt was it? "It had a Mandarin collar, a brocade bottom, and front ties."

Kimera is the future. It's where artists and businesses collide in a paragon of creativity and attractiveness. We need Kimera-like ventures in our churches and ministries.

### Community-Development Specialists: The Builders

Community-development specialists are the machinery, the builders, implementers, and directors of the ideas and enterprises dreamed up by the artists and entrepreneurs.

Critical to any community's sustainable transformation are the teams of people in any village or community or city that focus on education, housing, health, infrastructure, governance, relief, and spirituality. Without these teachers, doctors, builders, counselors, politicians, emergency aides, and spiritual guides, communities would fall apart.

In its studies of communities that are successfully transformed, World Vision highlights the importance of on-the-ground community-development specialists. They, along with businesspersons, are key contributors to the success of holistic transformation.

The world is tired of hearing the gospel preached by the church. They want to see it practiced by the church.

We, together, make up the church. We, together, all of us, are the priesthood.

In fact, Ephesians 4:11–16 (NLT) reminds us of the church leader's true role:

> He [Christ] is the one who gave these gifts to the church: the apostles, the prophets, the evangelists, and the pastors and teachers. Their responsibility is to equip God's people to do his work and build up the church, the body of Christ, until we come to such unity in our faith and knowledge of God's Son that we will be mature and full grown in the Lord, measuring up to the full stature of Christ.
>
> Then we will no longer be like children, forever changing our minds about what we believe because someone has told us something different or because someone has cleverly lied to us and made the lie sound like the truth. Instead, we will hold to the truth in love, becoming more and more in every way like Christ, who is the head of his body, the church. Under his direction, the whole body is fitted together perfectly. As each part does its own special work, it helps the other parts grow, so that the whole body is healthy and growing and full of love.

Our role as pastors and leaders in the church is to be the platform and, that difficult word to utter, a servant. I remember something else Max DePree said: "Leaders must build trust and bear pain." Our best work is not necessarily in the limelight of Sunday morning but in our private prayer spaces. It's in walking with someone in their hour of desperation. As pastoral leaders, our task is also to learn with the apostle Paul "to be all things to all men." We need to learn to walk in the blur and in the intersections of cultures, to bust the walls that separate us from a world of colliding cultures and generations, and the shifting of roles, responsibilties, and influence.

The apostle Peter clearly describes a church without walls in his first epistle:

> And now God is building you, as living stones, into his spiritual temple. What's more, you are God's holy priests, who offer the spiritual sacrifices that please him because of Jesus Christ. As the Scriptures express it,
>
> "I am placing a stone in Jerusalem,
> a chosen cornerstone,
> and anyone who believes in him
> will never be disappointed." . . .
>
> For you are a chosen people. You are a kingdom of priests, God's holy nation, his very own possession. This is so you can show others the goodness of God, for he called you out of the darkness into his wonderful light.
>
> "Once you were not a people;
> now you are the people of God.
> Once you received none of God's mercy;
> now you have received his mercy."
>
> —1 Peter 2:5–6, 9–10 NLT

## Past As Prologue

In his book *The Medici Effect*, Frans Johansson points out that this isn't the first time in history we have seen such a convergence of a small number of critical disciplines at a time of cultural upheaval.

Leonardo da Vinci is the illustrious standard-bearer of the Renaissance, a period when artists, scientists, and merchants stepped into the intersection of cultures and progress together and led one of Europe's most creative explosions of art, culture, and science. But the centuries that followed saw a growing specialization of knowledge. Disciplines became more fragmented, breaking into smaller and more specialized pieces. Today, however, that fragmentation is reversing and the effects can be seen in fields everywhere. Tom Friedman, foreign affairs columnist for the *New York Times*, in his book *The Lexus and the Olive Tree* comments on the growing connections in today's world: "Today, more than ever, the traditional boundaries between politics, culture, technology, finance, national security and ecology are disappearing."[11]

The blurring of lines and the upending of traditional walls has happened in each generation and will only increase in this one. It's really about learning to flow. Following the Jesus way of doing things. Just as in John 1, when we see the Son of God becoming man, the God of the universe allowing us to touch, smell, and see him, the living God. The work isn't the key thing as much as who we are. The work changes depending on the situation. Our calling remains the same: to glorify God by learning to flow with him. Our forms and styles will be varied and beautifully diverse.

> Few will have the greatness to bend history itself; but each of us can work to change a small portion of events, and in the total of all those acts will be written the history of this generation.... It is from numberless diverse acts of courage and belief that human history is thus shaped. Each time a man stands up for an ideal, or acts to improve the lot of others, or strikes out against injustice, he sends forth a

tiny ripple of hope, and crossing each other from a million different centers of energy and daring, those ripples build a current which can sweep down the mightiest walls of oppression and resistance.

—Robert F. Kennedy

current 7

# Ripples

> If you just learn a single trick ... you'll get along a lot better with all kinds of folks. You never really understand a person until you consider things from his point of view, until you climb inside of his skin and walk around in it.
>
> —Atticus Finch, in *To Kill a Mockingbird*

> Strange travel suggestions are dancing lessons from God.
>
> —Kurt Vonnegut

In the spring of 2003, a new fatal disease emerged onto the world's scene. It was known as SARS (severe acute respiratory syndrome). And when it broke out in China, traveling worldwide became restricted. This was a frightening global health threat, and the World Health Organization (WHO) recognized it had to act fast. And it did so by using the web, facilitating collaboration among the world's best experts. WHO connected scientists from fourteen countries and three continents to work together, in real-time, to share knowledge and test results. What happened? The unprecedented level of real-time networking led to the successful genetic mapping of the lethal virus in just thirty days. We have no excuse when it comes to collaboration because technology is so advanced and provides us with unprecedented tools.

Collaboration regularly takes place in the business world like it never has before. Boeing's newest jet, the 787 Dreamliner, was designed by a team of employees from seventy different companies around the globe. Many of the companies involved in the design project used to be regarded by Boeing as commercial threats.

The level, the degree, and the nature of collaboration are changing so rapidly. For us in the church, this is yet another major concern, because collaboration is something we've never really understood or done well.

Frans Johansson, in *The Medici Effect*, highlights an unlikely team of people from different cultures and disciplines who were responsible for cracking one of the most difficult ciphers used in World War II, the famous Enigma code devised by Germany. Thanks to the use of this shrewd code, during one year of the war, the Germans destroyed something like fifty Allied ships and submarines a month, killing tens of thousands of crewmembers. The Allies seemed helpless against the Enigma code, and traditional code-breaking methods had led to dead ends. So the British secretly gathered a diverse group of people in a mansion called Bletchley Park and put them to work on cracking the code. And they did crack the code, playing a major role in reversing the fortunes of the war for the Allies which eventually led to an armistice.[12]

The main argument that Professor Johansson makes in his timely book is that, if you look at history, it's undeniable that diversity, especially cultural and ethnic diversity, is a huge asset when it comes to innovation, creativity, and problem-solving. It just makes sense, doesn't it? It stands to reason that diversity brings forth fresh viewpoints, approaches, perspectives, learnings, ideas, insights, and sensibilities, and these in turn lead to breakthroughs, whether it's an opportunity we're trying to take advantage of or a problem or crisis we're trying to address.

### An Intersection: A Third-Culture Rountable Discussion

In the spirit of cross-cultural collaboration, we gathered some innovative colleagues and friends from around the globe for a freewheeling roundtable discussion on the topics we've been exploring in this book. Besides myself, the following people participated:

**Brennan Manning**, born in New York (christened Richard Francis Xavier Manning), is an author, friar, priest, contemplative, and speaker. One quote he's known for is, "The greatest single cause of atheism in the world today are Christians who acknowledge Jesus with their lips and walk out the door and deny him by their lifestyle. That is what an unbelieving world simply finds unbelievable."

**Jim Gustafson** is a lifelong community-development specialist and church-planter, and the son of missionary parents in Laos and Vietnam. Jim is considered by some to be the most significant missionary in Asia today. He is the third-culture Yoda! He has spent the last twenty-seven years planting churches in Thailand

and innovating contextualized ministry in Asia. Once considered a heretic by many in his generation, he has become a model for many progressive missionaries.

**Dave Brubaker**, a suburban-raised white brother, is a tattooed, bearded, modern-day bohemian, a University of California, Berkeley, graduate, and a global church-planter who works with the arts community in London.

**Benny Yu**, a Korean–South American reared in Paraguay and now living in Mexico City, is a tech-savvy businessperson and musician who works on behalf of orphans, child prostitutes, and marginalized people groups.

**Adam Edgerly** is an African-American executive coach and pastor of a multiethnic church in Los Angeles.

**Mehta Kriengparinyakij**, a next-generation leader in Thailand, is currently a teacher and musician.

**Steven Peters**, a young godly Indian-American living in India, is the CEO of a large education and community-development enterprise with plans to continue growing globally.

**Yo Warong**, a gifted Thai, is an anointed leader in Thailand who does community-development work and is a pastor in Bangkok.

**Jamie Strombeck**, one of our few representatives of the white community, loves Indiana basketball and the Chicago Cubs, has an MBA, and has worked as a missionary and community-development partner in Africa, Laos, and Bangkok.

**Patricia and Peter DeWitt**, both Canadians, are a passionate and phenomenal team working in Southeast Asia for more than fifteen years. They now pastor a third-culture church.

This is a diverse group of people in terms of culture and age (from twenty-six to eighty), and we probably don't even want to get into the vastly different temperaments, personalities, and sensibilities of this motley bunch.

What we have in common is we've practiced, and continue to practice, Jesus-focused ministry on every major continent. We love the gospel. We love the church. We believe in her. We want to see her thrive into the next century. To that end, we believe the third-culture way of thinking about and doing church can make a substantial contribution.

When we finally corralled everyone, we dove right in, taking up topics such as the condition of the church, the future of the church, the impact of globalism, and the power of third-culture concepts. What you see here is an edited version of the conversation. In a couple of instances, quotations came from one-on-one interviews, essentially separate continuations of the roundtable discussion with a couple of our global crew who couldn't make the roundtable but wanted to take part in the discussion.

### *Topic 1: The Third-Culture Concept*

**Mehta Kriengparinyakij**: To me, the soul of third culture is to celebrate the diversity of people and to serve diverse people—people who don't look like you, don't act like you, don't talk like you, don't live like you.

**Adam Edgerly**: And by being a third-culture church, we're saying that we as a church are going to intentionally cultivate that in ourselves.

**Brennan Manning**: It is so much the mind of Jesus—that we live together as brothers. All of the prejudices we've set up among cultures, among peoples of color, among backgrounds is so alien to the mind of Christ that it is the deepest kind of evil that I know.

Would this be a parallel? Three streams, one river—Asian, African-American, Caucasian all living, worshiping together, benefiting from one another's backgrounds. My enthusiasm to be enriched by, say, the music of the African community, your willingness to be enriched by my understanding of grace. Take all the cultures that come together and say, first, there is an openness to learn from one another. There is a desire to do it, and the thing I would add would be to sign a written statement that I would be willing to die, I am willing to give up my life, for this culture, for your culture.

I know of an American-based Christian group called the Micah Challenge. They go to Iraq, they go to Iran, and they go to Darfur. No weapons. They sit. They listen. They say, "What can we do to help?" And if they are captured or arrested (fourteen of them have already been murdered), they will seek no assistance from the United States government to be set free. But there's urgency and seriousness to this. As a Christian I have to ask myself, How willing am I to spend my time, my money, and my life in bringing about a third-culture movement?

**Jim Gustafson**: I have a friend who is a Muslim living in a Muslim community in Bangladesh. It's a very Muslim community, and if you ask him, he would say he is Muslim. But if you ask, Do you believe in Jesus Christ? "Yes." What has Jesus done for you? "He has saved me by his grace." And this guy is symbolic for me of what Jesus was about. We are not here to fight religions or religious battles. And we are not here to fight cultures or cultural battles. We are here to move in with the power of the love of God. That's beyond culture and beyond religion. We get so hung up on our own words and our own methods or ways of doing things.

My own life is an example. I lived twenty years as a missionary kid, and I was one of the best missionary kids around, and yet I didn't know Jesus Christ. But I was a Christian, because I was a missionary kid. Well, I was in seminary, and I was twenty years old when I truly came to know the grace of God and actually had a conversion experience.

I was studying Greek for a summer session at Fuller my last year, and I got down and I wept for three hours one night because I looked at Ephesians, and somehow God's grace came alive, through Greek of all things. And I thought, "If this is true, then this is the best thing that I have heard in my entire life!" Because I had always been performing for God. God just broke through to me. I do get comfort from the fact that Christ wasn't even a "Christian," so in fact it was okay for me to move from being culturally Christian to understanding and believing in God's grace in Jesus Christ.

But I have been on an odyssey ever since then, trying to somehow share the grace of God. That grace comes through in power as it is enculturated within a specific cultural context. People who are Muslims and Buddhists are finding their completion in Jesus Christ.

**Dave Gibbons**: Jim, some are concerned you might sound universalist. But I know you're a strong follower of Jesus Christ. What you're advocating here is beautiful. Our job is not to change the culture of people but to love them where they are. Let the Holy Spirit change them or point out where their culture comes in conflict with Christ. So many times we focus on forms and rules and miss out on loving people. I can maintain my convictions and core beliefs without manipulating or forcing people to maturity. I still remember that example you shared of the Buddhist priestess who came to know Jesus and had idols in her house. You didn't scold her about it right away. But you loved her and discipled her. One day you came back and they were all gone! You asked what happened, and she shared with you that God told her to get rid of them.

### *Topic 2: Crisis in the Church*

**Brennan Manning**: In the San Francisco Bay Area, the Methodist, Presbyterian, Nazarene—the leaders of all these denominations got together, they did a demographic study, and they found that *five* percent of Christians in the Bay Area went to church on Sunday. They also found out that young people cannot relate to a traditional service, so they began to do emergent stuff. But to me, the attitude toward what I would call the institutional church is about as negative as it has ever been. And I say that across the board about all the denominations because I speak in such a variety of churches. Unfortunately, they seem to be more interested in perpetuating the local church than proclaiming the good news of Jesus. So it's a very dark scene, as far as I am concerned, in my travels.

**Jamie Strombeck**: I feel like in the missions community, with the denomination I was in for a long time, it was kind of about us, because we've been around for fifty, sixty, seventy years and part of what we did, why we did it, how we did it, was keeping that organization going.

**Brennan Manning**: Well, in my lifetime, this is the most shameful time to be an American and to be a Catholic. It is a blood-drenched decade. It's a blood-drenched civilization. It's a blood-drenched country. For the love of Jesus Christ, how could we have allowed this to happen? The situation I see in the church is highly polarized.

I do share the concern about the megachurches. They are so preoccupied with comfort, convenience. Do you really think we need a bowling alley? How about a five-star restaurant?

I have a friend, Mrs. Brennan. She belongs to St. Dennis Catholic Church in New Orleans. She has been going there for thirty-eight years, and when she fell and broke her hip, she didn't know one person in that entire church to call for help. It's an absolute lack of community. And community, to me, is built by, "Okay, let's you and I go out and ring doorbells and find out who doesn't have enough to eat, who needs a ride to the doctor." The essential thing is that nobody in this church, or nobody in this neighborhood, ever goes to bed hungry. We are taking it upon ourselves, the responsibility of not only ringing doorbells but finding out, Is there anybody who is going to bed hungry? Is there anybody in this neighborhood who needs to go to a doctor and can't get a ride? Is there anybody in this neighborhood who, because of lack of medical insurance, cannot get the medical care they need?

To me, the lack of credibility of the Christian church in America is that we are not professional lovers of God and people. We've got this carrying of the Bibles, saying, "Praise Jesus!" and we don't love one another. We don't reach out and extend ourselves. Tell me the amount of money in your local church that is devoted to, first, the quality of faith of the people and, second, the assistance of the poor. Tell me those two things and I will tell you what I think of your church.

**Dave Brubaker**: This is a sad story. This person I'm very close to had a leadership meeting at this model church that many respect in America. The cool thing then, and it still is, was to emulate the business model. You know, to think of the senior pastor as the CEO, and the organizational structure is so corporate. And even today in the church, we are reading all the business books because we are trying to be so cool, when actually we should be the ones teaching them about leadership, right?

Anyway, he's in the middle of one of those leadership meetings and there are 120 people in the room, and the leader of the discussion is like, "So when you think about characteristics of a leader, what types of things are we talking about? If you are thinking about a leader you want to serve under, what are we looking for?"

Now, it was quiet; nobody was volunteering to say anything. And you know what you are supposed to say in that setting. You are supposed to describe some kind of a visionary, right? That is like the number one answer.

The dude up front calls on him because he is like, "Oh, _____________ is not shy; he'll throw out an answer." And so, without thinking—he should have known better—this person I'm close to said, "Loving?"

There was the most awkward silence in the room you have ever heard. The guy in front leading the session has this brutal moment where you can see he doesn't even want to write what he said on the board. You could just tell he was looking for a top five answer and he had just given an answer that was like number 172 in the discussion leader's mind.

It's hilarious looking back on it now, but I promise you, he felt completely humiliated at the time. I'll never forget it.

You always think about Jesus with stuff like that—like John 13:34–35, where Jesus says, "I am giving you one command: Love one another. They will know that you are my disciples by your love for one another." Jesus says that's the defining thing. It's not, "They will know you by your programs, your corporate imitations; they will know you by your worship." None of that! He is saying that people should be able to walk into the room and know that they have never seen so much love. People who see us should be going, "What is this? Oh, you guys must know Jesus, because there is no other love like this in the world."

### *Topic 3: Other Big Issues Facing the Church*

**Brennan Manning**: I think maybe the most demonic force that is afflicting the church is busyness. In the San Francisco Bay Area study, because of the cost of real estate, both parents have to work. Saturday is a day for household maintenance and shopping. And Sunday is the only day with the children. They don't go to church. That kind of busyness.

In this new book I am writing, the number of youth pastors and senior pastors who are on the run from God because of busyness is striking. They do not have any kind of an authentic spiritual life, and their life has become their ministry.

**Dave Gibbons**: When we were launching Newsong, I'd heard about all these burned-out church-planters. They're entrepreneurs, right? They're starting new churches, they're working like dogs, and they're killing their families. I just went to the Lord and said, "God, I can't do that. I don't know if you want that of me—to burn out for you. But that just doesn't make sense to me." I struggled with that whole thing. It's about burning on, not burning out.

Whenever I talk to pastors, you can see it in their eyes. They're dying. And I'm just looking at them, saying, "I know where you are. Whether I'm bigger than you or smaller than you, I know what you're dealing with."

Unless there's some type of rhythm of rest and restoration and relationship in our lives—and this is critical in the third-culture concept because of the intensity of loving someone not like you—I don't know if many of us can finish well. I hear the shop talk. It's not really from the Lord if we're just really trying to drive it. And again, I know this because I'm there. It's not because I'm different. It's because I've been there, and I have a tendency to go there. I think a lot of the paradigms and the philosophies that have guided us, even though they may come from a good heart, have taken us down a destructive road.

One leader I spoke to recently looked road weary. But you can feel the excitement in his voice as he talks about the seminars he's leading and how fast his church is growing. But I looked him in the eye and asked, "Are you burning out?" "Yes!" he replied. "And what about your people?" I asked. He jokingly said, "They are too, but we make them think they are having fun!" While I know my friend was kidding, I wondered whether it wasn't too far from reality when it comes to growing bigger or "healthier" churches.

**Dave Brubaker**: There's this classic moment in Martin Luther King's life that I love. There was this guy that was really opposing King and his people and blockading the movement, and the guy just said, "Look, I don't like what you guys are doing. I know you are trying to move forward, but you are not going to pass."

So King gets together with his guys, they have like a leadership team, and everyone is like, "Oh, this guy is such and such and this and that"—they're complaining and saying all these reasons why this guy is never going to do anything but be a problem. Well, Martin Luther King goes, "Does anyone have anything good to say about this man?" And King goes, "This meeting is adjourned until someone can find one thing that is good, because if you can find that point, that will be the place where God opens the door for us to continue forward."

They go out, and they do research, and it turns out he is a Catholic guy and has this great relationship with his priest. And they engage the priest as the one to go to him and say, "Look, you have got to see the merits of this movement." And that ended up being the door that allowed them to get in and move forward.

I think the church does the same thing with the world. It's a Genesis 1 worldview versus a Genesis 3 worldview. That's the biblical picture. If you choose to live in a Genesis 3 world, you see the world as cursed, bad, fallen. You are going to be looking around and saying, "Look at all the materialism in the world; people are so selfish and indulgent, and the world is full of sin."

If you live in a Genesis 1 world, you go, "Okay. Right. All that's there. And I can see that. But we still live in a Genesis 1 world too, where God says, 'It's good.' And especially when it comes to people, it's very good." But the church tends to walk through the world and pronounce a curse. That's all we see. Can we even see anything other than that? I don't know. But you know what? That's the easiest thing in the world to do. Anyone can do that. It's so cheap and easy to do the cynical thing, to tell you all the things that are wrong with it.

How about our being the ones walking around this world with Genesis 1 eyes and finding what's good in it? There is a miracle that happens when we choose to pronounce a blessing.

### *Topic 4: Third-Culture Ministry Movements*

**Adam Edgerly**: I will give you a story. A young woman at our church, an African-American woman with two teenage boys, got breast cancer. The guy who was leading our men's ministry, who is an Asian guy in medical school, got on the email list, sent out an email broadcast to the men's group, and brought a group of men, primarily Asian but a mixed group of men, over to her house. They cleaned up and renovated the house, sent the boys to Disneyland, and basically took care of this woman when she came back to make sure she didn't have anything else to worry about except her health.

When I see that kind of stuff happening spontaneously—nobody told them to do it; there is nothing going on in the pulpit; there is no sign-up sheet going around on Sunday morning; it is just one believer who says, "This has to happen!" And it is happening.

That is like Jesus with the Samaritan woman. You are crossing gender, age, ethnic, socio-economic, and educational barriers to reach out and love. It is happening. I wish it were happening more, but it is definitely happening, and it's organic. It's just the life of Christ. What I think we did, and what we are continuing to try to do, is to facilitate people coming together that way—where we set up a table and preach the gospel and see what happens.

**Dave Gibbons**: When you place yourself in the intersection of cultures—just like Professor Johansson talks about in

*The Medici Effect*—then new ideas and new things emerge. So we have trips where we place people in different cultural contexts that they are not used to. They actually start to adapt. They also see their own ideas and beliefs, how they are contrary to another culture around them, and it helps them become enlightened. That's a great experiential way to help move people toward this full embrace of the other.

**Benny Yu**: We are down in the southern part of the city next to the National Autonomous University of Mexico, and there are about three hundred thousand students. People from all over the world, especially Latin America, come and teach there. There's this one Cuban professor who teaches psychiatric courses. One of our guys, Jacob, got to know him and invited him to one of our barbeques.

Food is a great thing for meetings. And when there is free food, there is an even greater place for intersections. So we've just been inviting people for food. And because our ministry team is so multiethnic—we have one African-American, Jacob is Chicano, I am Asian, and then Cassie, she is Anglo—well, we just happen to draw a very multiethnic cross section of people. And those "Medici effect" moments just happen.

We had one party where the Cuban professor was there the whole time. He's an older gentleman, and as he left, he said to us, "You have no drugs at this party. You have no alcohol at this party. But there is a high in this place, and it's the friendships here and the people connecting with one another." And I said, "The funny thing is, quite honestly, more than half of these people just met today." So he left with almost a sense of joy, but also this confusion at the same time because of what he had experienced.

For us, when we talk about the importance of being third culture, we talk about how we need to cross borders and barriers to be able to experience God at a deeper, more intimate level, and maybe in a fresh way. It was cool for the Cuban professor because, as he was leaving, he got emails and phone numbers from people.

**Dave Gibbons**: There is a taste of heaven in that. That's the kingdom of God.

**Dave Brubaker**: We have talked about the whole conversion experience the church has prescribed, and how that maybe needs to be deconstructed. In our respective places around the world, what we're learning is just the power of showing honest, authentic love and concern for people. As we have been doing that, the response has just been so positive. It's intoxicating for people, and they taste it and they like it. But we often go, "Okay, make sure you sign and fill out this form," or, "Make sure you say this prayer." What we're seeing in London is we can trust completely in God and in his Spirit to be able to work in that person's life in a much more powerful way than we ever could.

**Jim Gustafson**: Yes. In South Thailand, we had touched the hearts and the minds of two women who were HIV/AIDS affected. One of them, the feistiest one, recently died. The one that wasn't so feisty is still living. And she now has spread her influence throughout the southern part of Thailand. With our help, her love and concern for people suffering in those HIV/AIDS communities has impacted communities in six provinces. And in Thailand HIV/AIDS creates suffering communities—they become social rejects even to their own families. They can't do anything to help themselves because they are HIV/AIDS affected.

I sat there at one of her meetings, and there were twenty some people in the room that day, and I was blown away because I didn't really expect anything. I expected to meet this one lady that was there. Well, six of the twenty had come to believe in Jesus Christ, not because they had been pushed but because they had been loved into it. And in turn, four of the six have their own communities where they are touching the lives of other HIV/AIDS-affected people. So they are a very impacted group, suffering themselves, but they are touching the lives of other people who are suffering.

But at the meeting, I did such a stupid thing. I sat there and I looked at them and I thought, "Gosh, what an opportunity to bring them to Christ!" And I know that Christ is already there, right? I understand that theology, that third-culture principle, and I try to live by it. But I made a stupid mistake and I looked at it the wrong way that day. All these rejected, suffering people in the room, and I asked, "What are you doing to bring these other people to Christ?" And the leader looked back at me and said, "Jim, how could you ask that? It's not my job to bring them to Christ. It's his job." He went on and said, "Jim, my job is to live the love of Jesus Christ that brought me to him in their presence. They have to voluntarily accept or reject Christ, but I have got to live it out." I thought, "I can't even live it out in this man's presence here today and he's this marginalized, impacted person who has all this suffering, and yet he's living out God's grace within his own community." I was blown away. Here's my resulting question: How can I enable people, in the context they are in, to have the freedom to accept Christ not just based on my Christian, cultural, and religious preferences but based on a true relationship to Jesus?

**Dave Gibbons**: And in a third-culture way, love them in the midst of our pain.

**Adam Edgerly**: I remember when we first started in LA, we would go to poetry readings and poetry slams. And the crowd was like the most densely populated, multicultural, multiage, multiethnic thing you'd ever see. You had these people sitting shoulder to shoulder, hundreds of people packed in these little rooms. I remember just looking around the room and thinking this is about the broadest cross section of humanity you could cram into a room.

And they had all these different styles, but they'd get up and just spit poetry. And the environment was very positive, very supportive, no matter what people get up to say, you know, everyone would just snap their fingers. Especially if someone said it was their first time, they'd just get nothing but love. Well, we would go to those places weekly and hand out cards saying this church is a place you guys would feel at home.

Art itself transcends culture and it brings people together. The content of the poetry usually had to do with life experience, the pain, the common denominator of pain and struggle, and it tends to unite people of all different cultures. At our church in LA, I'm finding that the whole emphasis on globalization, multiculturalism, the idea that the world could come together and peacefully coexist is attractive to people, and the church is often seen as an impediment to that. So when they find a Christian talking about this and saying, "No, this is something that God values, that God is intentionally doing," and that there's a place and a home for people who feel that way, it sort of validates what people are already attracted to today.

The other thing is I think the number of third-culture people in the world is increasing. So the percentage of people who don't feel comfortable isolated within their culture of origin is increasing. So they get fascinated when they find that somebody is talking about that as a positive thing and that a church is intentionally trying to create a home for people like that.

What I see in third culture is that it fits with a deep, deep biblical principle that needs to be recaptured. There's a mandate to do this. It isn't even optional in the gospel. The gospel is pushing us not just to associate with one another but to not look down on people. Paul says that you don't just spend time with each other, but you actually let the other person change you, to the point where in order to reach them for Jesus, in order to be in fellowship with them, they have to become like you, and you have to become like them. It's allowing the other person to change you. That is a deep, way-below-the-surface kind of reconciliation.

**Yo Warong**: When Newsong started in Bangkok, I remember I went to the leadership group meeting. And I met all the people, and I remember thinking, "Everyone is so crazy! Not normal; these are all abnormal people." Not crazy like mentally crazy, but crazy like when they start sharing, start talking, I feel very deeply connected to them. It was very easy. They felt like my family. I think when they speak, when they talk, there is something there. Because I had gone to many church groups, leadership groups, and all they talk is knowledge. But when these people talk, they say nothing about Bible. Sometimes, maybe. But they carry some love and they share their stories.

At the very first meeting, I remember they said, "Let's start with the pain in your life." Well, this was very different. In Thailand, in church, this is one thing that you can't ask, because people don't dare to share their pain or their life. You would just get to know them only by name or by what you are doing, the surface. But they start with, "Hey, can you share your pain or a hard time in your life," or something like that. I was like, "What!?" And they led the sharing; they started sharing one by one themselves. I remember that someone cried, and as they listened to each other's stories, they cried with each and prayed for each. I remember thinking this was the thing that I had always been looking for.

To be yourself and feel love, and they hug me and make me feel at home—I never feel like this in church, you know.

**Peter DeWitt**: Yes, one of the things that drew me to Newsong in Bangkok was the humility, the transparency.

I was a missionary and a pastor, but I always had this nagging feeling, "I'm a mess! My family is a mess!" My marriage was a mess. My kids were struggling with certain things. Inside, I am always thinking that I am a lousy person and an okay preacher and I do pretty good on Sunday morning, but for the rest of the week, I'm a complete mess. I am striving, praying, doing my devotions, and always there was this nagging feeling like I want to be honest. I want to be open about being messed up. I want to be real. I want people to know that I have problems. I've felt that our own denomination and church had become more and more policy-driven, top-driven, and rules-driven. But in Newsong Bangkok, I felt such a grace in the place.

**Jamie Strombeck**: I wanted a church where prostitutes, homosexuals—anybody that would normally never go into a church—would set foot into ours, and that's what it was in Bangkok. I was like, "Yeah! This is my joint. I am in church right now."

I am seeing God's Spirit working.

I am seeing a young Thai couple who are having marriage problems—they have been in debt, and their need is being answered by a Thai woman who's given them an interest-free loan to move them forward financially and in their marriage.

I am seeing prostitutes come in and sit side-by-side at a worship service with missionaries who might not even know that they are prostitutes, and these women are making the transition out of that life, taking a huge pay cut, but just wanting a better, different life.

I have seen young men and women from all over who have been burnt by the church and have issues with the church, and they are starting to forgive.

**Patricia DeWitt**: Third culture embraces the fact that *we* don't bring God. And these are the things that I have been questioning.

For a long time now, I would sit in missions meetings and I would hear people—leaders—talking about their results and their goals and their objectives. And I would think, "Oh, yeah, I see; I'm the bait and these are the fish." And they're counting people and talking about their friends as if this was an acquisition. I felt that this was wrong. What if those friends knew you were counting them and you were reporting them as your successes? That is not so genuine, is it? I hear these things and I've wondered, Is there a different way?

Third culture just brings a whole new face to what missions is. And it takes away that word even—missions—because the word is too small.

Instead, it's God who is doing things, and if we open our eyes and ask him, "Open my eyes. Open the eyes of my heart so I can see what you are doing." It is not God telling us, "Go clean your room in Thailand," or, "Go build something there." It is, "Hey, I'm making something in the kitchen. Do you want to join me?" That is such freedom!

## A Simple Exercise

At the end of our roundtable discussion, there was a brief prayer, because afterward we all were going back to our places around the globe and who knew when we'd all be together again.

I want to share the prayer with you. But I also want to tell you that if there's one thing we're learning in all of the places we are doing ministry and church around the world, it is that freedom, the word that Patricia DeWitt focused on, resonates with anyone, and it works everywhere.

And really, why wouldn't it? I could be wrong, but I'm not sure there's a lovelier word.

And yet around the world people don't generally associate freedom with church and Christianity. Even people who are working in the church and who are Christians, if they are honest, might struggle to say freedom is truly a mark of the church, ministry, or even their personal lives. Again, I know, because I've been there. I still go there.

The Scriptures talk over and over about freedom.

> I will walk about in freedom, for I have sought out your precepts.
>
> —Psalm 119:45

> The Spirit of the sovereign LORD is on me, because the LORD has anointed me to preach good news to the poor. He has sent me to bind up the brokenhearted, to proclaim freedom for the captives and release from darkness for the prisoners.
>
> —Isaiah 61:1

> The Spirit of the Lord is on me, because he has anointed me to preach good news to the poor. He has sent me to proclaim freedom for the prisoners and recovery of sight for the blind, to release the oppressed.
>
> —Luke 4:18

> Now the Lord is the Spirit, and where the Spirit of the Lord is, there is freedom.
>
> —2 Corinthians 3:17

If you summarized why Jesus came, it was for our freedom.

The thing is that the church, which Jesus loves, is supposed to be the manifestation of Jesus to the world, which Jesus also loves. But somehow freedom isn't what people associate with the church.

It's not that there aren't hundreds, if not thousands, of churches doing wonderfully at being Christ to their communities. But it's undeniable that the church at large today is not perceived and experienced the way we'd all want it to be. This is especially true in the Western church, which through the years has been so influential.

Some of us thought it would be a helpful exercise to list the attributes of Jesus — especially those that people through the centuries have been so captivated by — and then list what the church at large is known for. Here is what we came up with:

| **Jesus** | **Church** |
|---|---|
| Freedom | Rules |
| Anger in the name of people | Anger in the name of principles |
| Bottom up | Top down |
| Mysteries | Answers |
| Incarnational | Formulaic |
| Loving | Judging |
| Sacrifice | Comfort |

| Blessing the community | Converting the community |
|---|---|
| Decentralized power | Centralized power |
| Letting go | Holding tightly |
| Community | Individuals |
| Slowness | Velocity |
| Pain | Safety |
| Rabbinical/relational | How to/programmatic |
| Socratic/discovery/ journey | Didactic/solutions/ destination |
| Meekness | Mightyness |
| Smallness | Bigness |
| Variety | Homogeneous |
| Humility | Pretense |
| Authenticity | Masks |
| Maturity | Infantilism |
| Every day | Sunday |

I don't know what your list would look like. But I can promise you that going through the exercise will likely prompt some spirited, worthwhile discussion and learnings.

What we are finding is that the fifteenth-century monk who observed that "Jesus is the hardest part of the Christian faith to understand and the most difficult part to keep alive" had discovered something profound.

But what we also are seeing is that third-culture axioms are helping us get closer to making the experience of church and ministry more like the list of characteristics in that first column. And for that, we are grateful and joyful, because getting here hasn't always been easy.

Each of the participants in the roundtable discussion has learned to flow in any culture that is different from their own and to become water instead of trying to save the fish. I love being with them everywhere we happen to meet up in the world, because they epitomize third-culture leaders, loving their neighbors in the midst of discomfort and unfamiliarity and even chaos and pain. May we discover and send out more people in ministry just like them in the months and years ahead.

### A Simple Prayer

Our prayer at the conclusion of our roundtable went something like this:

> Thank you, God, that you've shown us what love is.
>
> That it's not just something that is verbal, but that it's alive and incarnate.
>
> That it requires getting messy, dirty, and even bloody.
>
> We wonder what would happen, God, if we realized that surrendering to Jesus means we're going to be tested and be made uncomfortable.
>
> If we in the church could learn to see the beauty of chaos, because we're learning that the more chaos there is, the more it's about Jesus and not about us.

If we could be a part of movements, events, conversations, and moments in which, if we don't exactly know what is going on, we can be content in just trying to keep up with what you might be doing instead of pressing our own agendas.

If we could learn to stop whining, stop trying to be in control, and lead simply with a contagious, abnormal joy.

If we could be able to live out the gospel in the settings where you place us, no matter how dark or uncomfortable.

If, when we speak the gospel, our lives could make our words credible.

If we could play a part, the smallest of parts even, in helping this beautiful messy thing called the church discover new language, new symbols, new stories, and new forms, so she can reach this very new world we are all blessed to be living in.

# Conclusion

The journey of a thousand miles begins with but a single step.

—Confucius

"You were a million years of work,"
said God and his angels, with needle and thread.
They kissed your head and said,
"You're a good kid and you make us proud.
So just give your best and the rest will come,
And we'll see you soon."

—Sleeping at Last, "Needle and Thread"

I was born in Arizona, and one thing Arizona is famous for is its monsoon season. In the summertime, there's a dramatic shift in the high-altitude air known as the Bermuda High. That shift, combined with the heating of the surface sands of the Mojave Desert, creates perfect monsoon conditions.

Now, what comes before a monsoon rainstorm is a huge windstorm. In fact, if you are in the Aquila Valley near Phoenix when a monsoon is on its way, you can actually see the wall of dust rolling in from far away. It's like a mile high, and the dust will start kicking up, and then you start feeling this crazy wind before the water actually falls down from the heavens.

It's a powerful natural phenomenon to witness.

The monsoon storms remind me of a supernatural storm that took place about two thousand years ago. It was the birth of a movement that impacts the world to this day.

In the second chapter of Acts, we learn of the amazing community of faith that formed in the first century after Jesus' death and resurrection. What made this Acts 2 community of faith so powerful and so unique?

Well, the first thing I love about this account is that in verse 2 it says, "Suddenly a sound like the blowing of a violent wind came from heaven."

There's a picture of this mighty, rushing wind. You can see it coming. But then, not only can you see it coming, it envelopes you. You are caught up in it. You can't escape it.

This wind is the Holy Spirit. Anyone who travels can experience the force of these winds blowing in the East, West, North, and South. This is a historic moment in the church to make a difference unparalleled by what the church has seen before.

### Fire

In the Acts 2 passage, something else happens when the mighty, rushing wind comes in. In verse 3 it says, "They saw what seemed to be tongues of fire that separated and came to rest on each of them." Fire. A fire that came upon each of them. Maybe on their heads; I don't know exactly where it was. It could have been in their eyes. Have you ever seen fire in someone's eyes? I have seen it in the eyes of many of my spiritual mentors. They're often older. While they're usually becoming frailer physically, their fire burns brighter as they age. If you look into their eyes, you see lions and wild bulls. I see the same spark in young leaders with whom I have the privilege of doing ministry and church around the world.

One of the things that happens when the mighty wind of the Holy Spirit begins to blow, I believe, is that a fire comes upon us. You can see it in the eyes of an anointed leader. Do you have that fire? How can we get it?

I have to admit, even as recently as a couple of years ago, I felt the flame dimming. I was going through the motions of ministry but the zeal was gone.

Once during our church's history we lost a piece of land we were trying to buy. It was a dream piece of land, especially as it related to freeway access and visibility. The loss surprised me. It was an emotional letdown when the transaction didn't take place. Even to this day, I like to give the company that bought that piece of land a hearty boo when I pass by.

At the time, I thought for sure what was happening with our acquiring the land was something of God. So I took a serious nosedive when it all came crashing down. Whenever I drove by the land that was now occupied by the car company, I pretty much lost it. I told people, "Man, I want to picket that place." I told people, "Don't buy their cars, man."

During this whole time we were looking at the land, I kept making this little statement: "It's not about the land and it's not about the building; it's about what happens *in* the building." It was one of the best marketing lines that I have ever used in my life. And so what does God often do? God tests us on our statements, right? You know, when we say, "I surrender all of me to you, God," God says, "Do you really surrender *every*thing?" Or we say, "Lord, send me anywhere." Do you really mean *any*where?

After it all fell through, God spoke to me. God said, "Dave, it's not about the building, and it's not just about what happens *in* the building either. What matters most is how each person lives outside the church building." And I started thinking more deeply about that phrase. What I'd used as a marketing line or a rationalization or whatever, God began using for a whole different purpose. And I realized anew that neither any individual church nor the church at large is defined or bound by the house. It's about the home.

And I thought this truly might be the most significant sin and idol of the church, especially in America. We think it's all about the building because that affirms us, that's what indicates we've made it. It's the church version of the American Dream. But even as many traditional church buildings around the world are empty, I think God's saying, "No, I've got a different plan."

I think it's possible God's saying there is a building that I am trying to build that is not made with hands. It's made by the Holy Wind, the Rushing Wind of the Holy Spirit that breathes fire and life into individuals. And they will become the temple of God. And as these people become the temple of God, they will be living temples. And the beauty of these living temples is that they are not stationary. They don't have to all stay in one spot, and in fact I am going to scatter these living temples everywhere. And there are many domains, and whether it's an artists' village or a concert or a pub or an orphanage or a hospital or a school or a private residence, wherever these people can be, they will be a reflection of God's glory. And I've found myself starting to understand that God has a different building in mind for the church.

## Keep the Golden Ticket

I'm learning that, increasingly, in ministry and church, choosing to do what you think you are called to do can cause a lot of anxiety, stir doubts, and draw criticism, and that, at times — maybe even the majority of the time — you can look foolish. You might take some heat trying to do racial reconciliation and love the marginalized. While there are glorious moments when you connect with people of different cultures, it's painful to adapt to others who are not like you.

At our church, even as we've had more excitement than ever among our leadership and faith community as we've embraced third-culture thinking and ways, we've faced more financial pressure. Our church has always experienced financial shortfalls, but for some reason, it seemed to intensify as our vision sharpened and we started doing new ministry around the world.

For a while, this really made me nervous. I wondered why I was reacting like this, especially since we had been able to deal with it many times before, like most churches do. When we started Newsong, we had pledges of twenty-four thousand dollars, and that was it. But we didn't have nearly that much coming in. Our first offering was about five bucks, and I remember thinking that this church was not going to make it. In the beginning, I was using my credit cards, I was using my pension fund, and I was taking out credit. And if you did the math, it wasn't looking good when you saw what was coming in.

It's at that moment of desperation, not knowing where resources are coming from, that many will sell their golden ticket. They'll give up right before they strike gold.

One day I found myself watching the movie *Charlie and the Chocolate Factory*. The plot of the movie revolves around the fact that five golden tickets have been placed inside the wrappers of some of Willy Wonka's famous candy bars. And the five kids worldwide who buy the candy bars with the five golden tickets inside will get to meet Willy and enjoy a day inside the secretive chocolate factory.

Charlie, the lovable main character, comes from a family that is in rough shape financially; in fact, all four grandparents live with Charlie and his parents in this tiny, beat-up, one-room house. Well, Charlie gets the last golden ticket, and he runs home and he is so excited, holding it in his hand. His family is freaking out and they are so excited because they thought that it would never happen. And then Charlie stops and quiets himself. He says, "A woman in the store said that she would give me five hundred dollars for it, and they would probably give me more if I asked. We need the money more than I need a visit to the chocolate factory, so we have to sell it."

The crotchety old grandpa who is the most cynical and negative one of all pulls him over and says, "Charlie, the world is full of money. They print more every day. But there are only five of these tickets. You'd have to be a moron to sell it for something as common as money. You are not a moron, are you?"

Sometimes it's so simple we forget it, don't we? We cannot let worrying about something as common as money get in the way of our calling or mission or vision. A lot of times, I think obstacles like money are placed in our path to see how badly we want to accomplish something. Worrying about money never would have stopped me early in ministry, but for some reason I let it get the best of me for a while. Well, not anymore. The freedom I've gained in pursuing the vision God has given me for ministry with all my heart is beyond words.

Our church now is getting back on track, but we lost people and money because of our decision to be a third-culture church. Loving your neighbor comes with a cost. The pain is noticeable and often lasts longer than we want it to. People have asked me whether it was worth it to go to Thailand for a year, absorb these pains, and lose some long-standing members. I would do it again—a thousand times over! The third-culture journey is arduous and painful at times, but it is our golden ticket to loving God and loving our neighbor.

And by the way, God will sustain you. Today, as I finish this section of the book, I saw close to three hundred thousand dollars come into our church in the last twenty-four hours! We're above budget—for now anyway! Either way, there's no going back.

## Chaos Theory

If you walk into our home, it is usually beautiful. But many times it looks great only because we were going crazy cleaning our house ten minutes before you arrived. So if you go into our living room, it looks awesome, but please don't open our garage door, because, man, we are talking chaos! There is stuff all over the place; our kids have thrown their stuff, their laundry, here, there, everywhere. There are piles all over. For all I know, you could find dead people in there. It's our version of the Amazon jungle!

At home, we don't like to talk about the chaos, because we want everybody to think that we have it all together, that we are clean, that we have everything in its place. But the truth is sometimes we are struggling to keep up and things aren't all that together. And that's okay; it's part of the third-culture deal.

When I think about my garage, I realize I just need to learn how to embrace chaos better, because movements of God are marked by chaos. They are not systematic and orderly and clean. Why? Because movements of God are fundamentally movements about love, and there's very little that's predictable and orderly and clean about love.

Love is messy.

Love is chaotic.

Love is foolish.

Love is perilous.

Love is, as a song by Sleeping at Last says, tension and thrill.

You cannot put a box around a movement of God. You cannot expect everything to add up and be able to say the outcome is guaranteed. It's probably not going to make sense.

It's like trying to describe the Grand Canyon. It's beautiful. It's something to behold. There's an element of the miraculous about it. But no matter what words you use, you can't really do it justice. It defies description.

You know it when you see it, though.

Not long ago, a twenty-year-old man was waiting for a train in a subway station in New York City when he suffered a seizure. He fell onto the tracks just as a train was speeding into the station.

Standing nearby was a fifty-year-old construction worker and navy veteran named Wesley Autrey. Mr. Autrey was waiting for his own train, preparing to take his two young daughters home before work.

When he saw the convulsing young man suddenly collapse, Mr. Autrey rushed to the edge of the tracks and quickly sized up the situation. He could see the headlights of the train as it was about to enter the station and he leaped onto the tracks.

Quickly placing the young man between the rails, he lay on top of him to keep him from flailing and prayed there'd be enough clearance, because the train was traveling too fast to stop in time, even though the conductor tried.

Five cars passed overhead before the train stopped, the cars whizzing by so close to his head they left a smudge of grease on his blue knit cap. When he realized they were both fine, he yelled to shocked onlookers standing on the subway platform, "We're okay down here. But I've got two daughters up there. Let them know their father's okay." Applause broke out as witnesses marveled at the act of courage and love they'd seen.

Now I could be wrong, but I'm not sure there's a better picture of what movements of God are supposed to be about.

Today, there are all kinds of speeding trains coming at us in the church, all kinds of chaos, all kinds of unfinished stories. Let's embrace all of it. Let's not shrink from one bit of it. Let's not be the least bit afraid. We don't have to be. Instead, just as Mr. Autrey did, let's leap. Let's do the one thing we have been called to do. "Love as I have loved," Jesus tells us in John 15. "Put your lives on the line," he says.

### Dad

My dad passed away in February 2007, and in his final months, I flew back and forth a lot to Phoenix to be with him. I got to see the progression of my father—not just the progression of his disease but also the progression of his spirituality.

At the point when he found out that the disease might kill him, he got interested in the Scriptures, and he said,

"Dave, I have been reading the Bible." Before my dad left the church and before he divorced my mother, he had a love for the Bible. He was actually a very good Bible teacher.

I said, "You have? What are you doing?"

He said, "I am reading about five to ten chapters a day."

And I said, "What has God been saying to you?"

He said, "God has been telling me that I have been away too long." And he just started crying.

As time got shorter and my dad reached his last moments, I looked into his eyes and saw how he'd become a different person. He had been fighting for his life. And I told my father at the last moment, the last day that he was alive, "Dad, you have got to fight this thing. You have got to fight it. Come on, Dad, don't give up!" But my dad just said, "I can't. I can't." And then I saw tears in his eyes because he knew that he couldn't battle it anymore. The multiple chemo sessions, the burden he felt he was placing on his wife, and the excruciating pain became overwhelming for him emotionally and physically. He didn't have the will to fight anymore.

It was about eleven o'clock at night when he looked at me and said, "Dave, can you help me?" My dad was still strong even though his body was deteriorating on the inside. He took my arm and hoisted himself up. He pulled himself to look right at me where I was sitting in the chair next to his bed. He just gazed at me and I kept eye contact with him.

Then, I watched as his breath just got slower and slower and slower until he didn't take any more breaths and his eyes were still open looking right at me as he gently passed away.

When I did my dad's funeral in Phoenix, I hardly cried, because I felt like I had to be the brave one. So I didn't get a chance to mourn until a couple of weeks later. And one day, quite suddenly, I just started sobbing. I missed my dad so much.

These days, I think of my dad all the time because God reminds me of the worst and the best about the church through him.

The church exists, and Jesus came, so there'd be a place for people like my father, a guy who was rejected by the church because he had had an affair at one point in his life. Christians, even pastors, advised me not to deal with my dad. They told me to separate from my father, because he needed to know that what he did was wrong.

One reason I continue to try to live out the third-culture way is because I envision a church for people like my father—an ordinary guy with extraordinary burdens of shame and failure. The truth is that loving our neighbor is not just a cross-cultural experience but an experience of the cross. It's choosing to absorb the pain of others so that they can experience the love of the Father.

And the win for us? While we are loving our neighbors, we're actually loving God. And he's loving on us. The two commandments Jesus says we're to be about are really one. They're two sides of the same coin. You can't do one without the other. As the apostle John said, "if you can't love someone you can see, how can you love a God you don't see?"

That is the heart of God. And it is the dream of Jesus, I believe.

# Becoming Third Culture

## Practical Next Steps

One of the great challenges with a concept like third culture is how to apply it. This section will illuminate in a practical way some good next steps you and your church or ministry can take.

### Current 1: Liquid

Here are some things that have helped me and many others "become water" to those we serve anywhere in the world:

1. *Educate yourself* by reading authors of different cultures, political persuasions, and perspectives, even people you may fear. For example, I read work by

Malcolm X, and it changed my life. I was able to relate to his pain and could see how much of his communication was hyperbole for the sake of a larger point and the greater good. I remember seeing Malcolm X on TV when I was young and thinking, "Man, this guy's a radical. He's crazy." Then I got his biography and read Spike Lee's foreword, and when I read the book, I started crying, because then I understood him. I understood why he was so vitriolic. It was because he had lived in the context of consistent abuse and prejudice. It would make anybody angry. I read *Malcolm and Martin*, the study on Malcolm X and Martin Luther King Jr., how their lives converged, and how they moved toward greater understanding of one another as they got older. Then my curiosity was piqued. I started reading authors and thinkers from different circles and seeing biblically, theologically, how God cares so much for the outsider and how much that concept is ingrained in the Scriptures.

2. *Interview people* who are doing third-culture work locally and globally, people who are moving beyond the Sunday-morning choir-and-sermon experience and working through the pain, discomfort, and sacrifice of engaging someone radically different from themselves. I traveled to places in North America, Central America, and Asia. If cost is a factor, you might find that much of the world is already in your back yard, especially in the United States. There are so many

immigrant groups and international students even in the rural Midwest or the South. At one point, I went around the country and the world, especially to places of transformation like Chicago and Washington, DC, and interviewed leaders and practitioners. In Chicago, one amazing person I visited with is Coach, this white guy who works with African-Americans. He helped build this huge clinic and sports ministry in Illinois. And I went to El Salvador and saw rampant poverty and the destruction it always sows. And I learned how an entire, essentially broken international community was transformed in ten to fifteen years. A place of death became a place of hope. Go to these places, investigate, and learn.

3. *Experience the street.* We go on what we call vision trips, on which our main focus is to see what God is doing, to see the city or community through his eyes. We do prayer walks and then at night share what we felt and saw and what God might be saying to us. We pray the prayer that Bob Pierce, founder of World Vision, prayed: "Break my heart with the things that break your heart." Our church in Crenshaw, California, one of the murder capitals of the United States, started after a prayer walk there. One thing that really helped was to have Dr. Michael Mata, World Vision leader, to share with us how to exegete a city—how to spend some time in a city and see the cues that will tell you about the hopes and dreams, the struggles and pain of any city. He gave

us a perspective that helped us to identify both the pain and the beauty of any people group in any city. It's experiencing the street that has helped me the most.

4. *Befriend someone who is not like you*, specifically someone of a different culture. This could be an international student from your local university or your local campus ministry. If you're a pastor, consider mentoring someone from a local seminary or partnering with someone from an ethnic church. Take the initiative to approach someone who is not like you. Plan regular meals or coffees together.
5. *Attend networks, gatherings, or conferences that you usually wouldn't attend*, especially events that involve different denominations, ethnic groups, styles, flavors, and ages. After a while it's kind of tiring to keep attending the same homogeneous conferences and gatherings year after year. An intellectual and cultural incestuousness seeps in. Try something like the annual Urban Youth Workers Conference or their local initiatives in cities all across America. You'll form new friendships and gain a broader understanding of God.
6. *Get others involved*. While you may not want to immerse your whole community immediately, you can put together a strategy that includes education and experiences that will help your congregation move to a new level. You can check out several websites, including one we have developed, xealot.net.

## Current 2: Wardrobe

What is the true bottom line of transformation?

World Vision not only uses metrics but also ensures that it is operating in key domains that truly do transform a village, community, or city: health, education, housing, spirituality, clean water, and economic development, areas in which our churches and ministries can make a meaningful contribution. They are essential components as we do work in compassion, justice, and advocacy.

There is little chance that one church of any size, or one ministry or even one plan, can take care of the needs of a given community in these domains. We need to passionately pursue collaboration with local government, businesses, artists, health professionals, lawyers, athletes, educators, and other churches and nonprofits to be a part of a transformation team. One of our primary mantras is we don't care who gets the credit, especially if we really believe in the kingdom of God and in one church.

In Bangkok, a church was doing a music concert in the park and our group volunteered to serve them in their event. Our team told the other church's leadership team we would wear their church's T-shirts and serve as ushers, cleanup crew, and whatever else they needed at the concert. It was a beautiful demonstration of the reality that transformation requires a host of churches, leaders, and sectors.

Consider with your team what the stated and unstated metrics of life change are for your church in the community God has placed you in. Which ones, spoken or unspoken, do you care most about? Which ones do you think God cares most about in your place and time?

## Current 3: Neighbor

If loving your neighbor is going to be one of the main things you and your church and ministry are going to be about, it starts with you. What percentage of time can you give toward building relationships with those who are outsiders in your community? When you look at your planner and your schedule, how much time are you actually devoting to that? When you look at your church, how much time, money, and effort are you really devoting toward third-culture initiatives?

Locally, you can start out by first going to your community and government leaders and asking, How can our community serve you? Ask the locals, Who are the most underresourced people in the community? Where are the walls broken down? To create a vision, use the Nehemiah principle. Nehemiah, before he had the vision to rebuild the walls of Jerusalem in fifty-two days, first had to see the destruction and feel it and mourn it. So start meeting with leaders and learn who's most in need and whose voice is most neglected, sometimes just for lack of resources. Make this part of the time that you're devoting to building relationships with outsiders every week. If you're in a suburban area, make it a part of your life to venture into the urban centers near you, because that's often where the need will be greatest, and see where you could play a part, no matter how small.

On a global level, is missions ancillary, like a department? Or is it really at the heart of your church?

Pray about your local university and spend time with the international students there. If you're saying you don't see international people groups in your community, well, look at your campus and they'll likely be there. Students from all over the world still come to the United States for undergraduate and graduate education. So what do you do with them? Offering academic tutoring, classes in English as a second language, and classes in American culture are all helpful starting places.

### Current 4: Liquid Bruce Lee

Key third-culture concepts:

- Be water
- Love without strings attached
- Shift 1: from consumerism to cause-ism
- Shift 2: from pastor to social entrepreneur
- Shift 3: from paths to rhythms
- Christ, cause, community

Right near my condo in Bangkok was a British Country Club. A couple whom I had married in California were visiting family who had a membership there, and they invited me to go to the club with them. When I walked in, I noticed almost everyone was Western. It felt like I was in Europe or North America. I was home! They had a Western lunch menu and Western drinks. People all around me spoke English. People were playing tennis, and others basking in the sun by the pool with cocktails in hand. It was surreal because I felt like I was in California, but we were still in Thailand. Little did I know there'd be a valuable lesson for me in this scene.

When I first went to Bangkok, I was told by Jim Gustafson to be sure to adapt to the local cultures and customs. So, immersed in a new culture, I tried to be sensitive about my Western ways. I really wanted to make sure I respected the Thai culture. Moreover, on one of my visits prior to my move to Bangkok, I noticed that international churches there seemed to have few Thais among their community. I didn't want to make the same mistake. And then it struck me—the connection between the surreal scene of the British Country Club and the church. We in the church seem to do the same thing the country club did. We replicate places where we all drink the same Kool-Aid and hang out with people who are attracted to the same things we are. These communities tend to be exclusive and insular, but God has called us to become like water, to adapt to the currents where he is flowing.

Believe me, I know firsthand how challenging this can be. When we pulled off our first preview service in Bangkok, I thought it was a home run. We had a large crowd, dynamic preaching, great food, beautiful music. And all of this was contained in a brand-new facility. It was state of the art! We were in a cool new theater with new seats, lots of multimedia equipment, stellar acoustics, and even new paint. We finished the service on a high. Or so I thought.

I was ready to dive into the crowd of well-wishers who I felt would thank me for our first official service in a brand spanking new facility in a brand new country and culture. Well, the Thai leaders approached me with gentle smiles. They said they liked it, but they didn't feel it was Newsong. Trying not to show my shock or offense, I said, "What do you mean it didn't *feel* Newsong?" Meantime, I was thinking, "Hey, I founded Newsong, guys; I think I know what Newsong is!"

They told me, "Newsong is about community, not just a show where a few people serve and everyone else watches. When we sit in this new building, most of us are in these rows facing the stage. We're not interacting with one another so much as watching a few people on the stage perform. Thais like to face one another. We're about being a community where eveyone gets involved."

I came to my senses and asked them what form the Thais would love. They said, "Circles."

From that moment on, we started doing circles at every one of our gatherings. Even at our large meetings in Bangkok. Cognizant of contextualization, despite my best efforts, I had defaulted to a way of doing things that I grew up with but that didn't fit the context we were in.

To be water to the people God places us with, to smoothly flow with the currents God has already stirred in the places he sends us to, there are several key third-culture principles to consider:

1. *Listen* more than we speak. Americans, in particular, are known for our loudness and inability to listen respectfully and well.
2. *Believe* that the locals know more than we do and be eager to learn from them. They live there. We're visitors.
3. *Understand* that Jesus is already there. We're not bringing Jesus to them.

4. *Be open* to redeeming or giving new meaning to cultural practices or customs that we may not understand or even be comfortable with.
5. *Respect* the forms and practices of a given culture. Just as we are sensitive to learn the language of a foreign culture, so we must learn the nonverbal language of the culture.
6. *Recognize* that what is offensive to much of the world is Christianity, especially cultural Christianity, and not Jesus himself. Jesus is pretty irresistible to most people around the world and, in almost every case, is intriguing in the most positive way.

## Current 5: Three Questions That Become the Answers

I remember asking a pastor when I was in high school whether there are any gray areas in the Bible. He responded, "No, it's all black and white." I'm not sure what Bible he was reading, but there is a lot of gray. It doesn't mean God isn't clear on a lot of issues, but there are things we just don't know. There's a lot of paradox and mystery. But that's often hard for us to admit.

I came to realize over time that answers often depend on circumstances. For example, while you may have the liberty to drink wine, you might choose not to drink when you are with a Christian in the Bible Belt who would be offended by it. But when you are in Europe, you would feel free to have a glass of wine. The same is true when you deal with third-culture settings. Answers that work in Texas won't work in

Shanghai. But the three questions we discussed in chapter 5 will always lead us to a good place, no matter where we are.

1. Where is Nazareth?
2. What is my pain?
3. What is in my hand?

I've applied these three questions when I sense God is calling us to serve in a particular city or community. These three questions have helped us to launch churches in cities that wouldn't be the least bit interested in a cookie-cutter version of our Irvine location.

These three questions led us to start a church and a community-development corporation called the SHAW in the high-crime, high-poverty area near Los Angeles called Crenshaw. When point leaders in Los Angeles asked, What is our pain? the needs of single moms and their children as well as the need for artists to find their voices were the answers. For example, Cue, our iconic leader, shared his pain with the music industry. He had had a contract with a major record label, and they made millions of dollars off of him, but he saw hardly any of it. And family pain? He's seen his share with the absence of his father and the physical abuse he received when he was a child. You can still see the cigarette burns on his skin that a guardian etched on his arms. It was Cue's pain that really led us to start the SHAW, a community-development entity focused on Sports, Health, the Arts, and Whatever! Cue's pain became the platform for a lot of people's good. His pain is his street credibility.

## Current 6: cWoWs

As you learn to flow with who you are and what God is doing in you, you crave ways to make a difference. As the Scriptures say, "He who has been forgiven much, loves much." But if all there is to do in the church is within the four walls of our material structures, a lot of people are going to be left out.

I've helped to start several organizations and businesses in the fields of music, finance, and technology. I love it! When I started working more closely with my teammates in these three domains, I discovered that a lot of people in fields outside of religious academia or religious institutions feel like they are not really doing meaningful work, because they see professional religious work as the pinnacle of sacrifice. That grieved me. I had to do something about it.

Here are some things we did at Newsong at different locations around the world to blur the lines, to create a church without walls, engaging key people such as artists, businesspersons, and community-development specialists:

1. *We changed our language.* Instead of calling the staff pastors, we refer to ourselves as the support team. We call the members the field team.
2. *We changed the way we gave to missions.* Instead of one person or a handful of people deciding where all the money goes and being the relational connection to community-development specialists and missionaries, we developed what we call the Cause Investment Portfolio. Through this portfolio, people in the church

choose what and who they want to support, and they give to and interact with those causes directly. We've found that the community-development specialists and missionaries and the people in the church liked this better. It gives the people in the church more ownership and a greater level of involvement, relationship, and fulfillment. And it gives the people who are supported relationships with their donors. Both groups love it. In fact, this cause-portfolio concept birthed a revolutionary website that allows everyone to play when it comes to third-culture initiatives locally and globally. It saves pastors and congregations money and time. Check it out at http://yangdang.com.

3. *We changed our website.* We're evolving our website from a content-driven, events-driven site to a social-network site focused on developing our faith community locally, regionally, and globally. It's essentially a customized social-network site that serves all of the people around the world in our faith community. Our community can post videos, blogs, and events directly without having to go through professional staff. It's a dynamic, not static, site.
4. *We became third-culture multisites.* We are still one church, but each site is now a separate legal entity to foster ownership, yet we still come together in areas where we're better served together than apart. These sites are not franchised clones but are adapted specifically to their urban or suburban location globally, yet still have a third-culture priority. Our sites' areas of

intersection are primarily leadership development, creative resources, and missional initiatives.

### Current 7: Ripples

Consider hosting your own third-culture roundtable discussion. Invite leaders from different cultural backgrounds, demographics, faith traditions, and socio-economic backgrounds and ask them some questions. Eat together. Hear each other's stories. Record the discussion and give everyone a transcript. You'll become part of a beautiful mosaic that will inspire greater creativity, innovation, and understanding in your church.

I met with a Coca-Cola executive recently who shared with me that one of the great things they do with their international crew is bring their top regional executives together simply to share best practices. Whoever wants to collaborate after the meeting has further sidebar conversations. Many great synergies and collaborations have occurred from that initial collaboration. The best innovations often come from the fringe. Regularly fuel the fringe while still honoring the past.

Consider sponsoring something like that. Provide a great meal and a time frame of maybe ninety minutes to two hours and see what happens. Limit the size of the group to five to twelve people so everyone can talk. You can network, build friendships, and possibly do something greater together than what you could do by yourself. You don't have to be friends with everybody; you simple need to see the benefit in getting together with people who are different from you. I do this all the time. In fact, one of the other reasons I started Xealot was to foster this type of interaction among artists, businesspersons, and community-development specialists. I felt that as a pastor, I needed this interaction. I see some of these people regularly, and some I call almost every day to be encouraged, to be inspired, and to join forces with to do the work of transformation.

### Conclusion

When your church grows, you get criticized for a lot of things. Maybe some of it is legitimate. One myth is that large churches lack spiritual depth. It's assumed that if you're big, you're not deep. But you can be small and have similar issues too. Here's a solution for the lack of depth and spiritual maturity in our churches, whether they're big or small. It's not another Bible study or a spiritual "to do" task, because the solution is more relational and lifestyle driven. The best thing we can do to know Christ more deeply and to make a difference with our lives is to be third culture. Have the mindset and will to love, learn, and serve in any culture, even in the midst of pain and discomfort. It's a being choice. As we love our neighbors who are not like us, we come to know Jesus, and we find our closest taste of heaven on this earth.

Be water, my friend.

# On the Verge

## An Interview with David Gibbons

Author's Note: In a *Leadership* journal article, I was asked about the third-culture journey I've been on. This appendix is a reprint of that article.

*David Gibbons had an unlikely education for someone who would pastor a multi-ethnic church. Growing up in a fundamentalist church, he attended one of fundamentalism's flagship schools, a university with a policy at that time against inter-racial dating. "There were many great things about the school," he says. "The speech and arts programs were phenomenal, the academic standards were high, and they had a lot of*

"On the Verge: An Interview with David Gibbons," *Leadership* 29, no. 3 (summer 2008), 72. Reprinted with permission of *Leadership* journal.  www.leadershipjournal.net.

*women! I thought my chances were pretty good." But David was quickly informed of the school's policy against inter-racial dating. "I complicated things for them," said David, "because my dad was white; my mom was Korean. I'm inter-racial!" The school told him he had to choose between Caucasian or Asian. He couldn't date both. Eventually David met the woman there who would become his wife. She is Caucasian and American Indian. Today David is pastor of NewSong Church, which he planted in Irvine, California, in 1994, with multi-site locations in Los Angeles, North Orange County, Dallas, Mexico City, London, India, and Bangkok. Andy Crouch and Marshall Shelley interviewed David about how his understanding of the gospel has grown and developed.*

**What part did your carefully segregated college experience play in your calling and ministry?**

Looking back on that whole experience, I always ask, "Why did God take me through that?" I think he was preparing me, actually, for the way we do church around the world.

**That's a surprising twist on the story.**

Ethnic churches have their own forms of prejudice. It's not talked about much. It's okay for people of other ethnicities to come to the church and sit there. But when it comes to marrying my son or dating my daughter, there's hostility.

The Asian church was unfamiliar to me—I had grown up in a white, majority culture church. But some mentors encouraged me to explore the Asian part of my heritage. So I attended a Korean church that was known as the premier church on the East Coast at the time, and I saw the children bored during service. I had never before experienced that.

I'd been raised in a fundamentalist church that kept it lively and fun. And I thought, *Hey, things should be a little more engaging than this.* I realized that if the leading Korean church is having trouble retaining their second generation, this must be going on all across America. So I joined the staff of a Korean church in Dallas. I fell in love with the people, but also experienced the heartaches of second-generation issues—the so-called "silent exodus."

All these experiences caused me to examine my life and who I was, my biracial background, my heart for the globe and not just one culture.

**Where did that examination lead?**

When I visited California In 1993, I sensed God saying something. In a hotel room, I heard two words: "Psalm 40." I heard it twice, and I looked it up: "I waited patiently for the Lord; he ... heard my cry. He brought me up out of the pit ... out of the miry clay. He set my feet upon a rock, making my footsteps firm. He put a new song in my mouth, a song of praise to our God; many will see and fear, and will trust in the Lord."

I felt an urging to move to California. It was crazy, because we had just bought a house, but we moved. We sold everything, moved to Orange County, and launched NewSong Church in 1994.

**What influences shaped NewSong?**

We had a vision of multi-ethnicity and ethnic reconciliation and reaching the next generation. The country was still reeling from the L.A. riots, and the need for a church like this was obvious. We were also influenced by the church growth principles that were so important in the 1990s. And our church experienced rapid growth.

It started taking off, which was great. But the problem with rapid growth is it's very hard to reflect deeply. You're juggling twenty balls, and you're just trying to keep up with small groups, community life, the various crises that come along.

About ten years into NewSong, I began to be dissatisfied. I was in the middle of a funding campaign—I don't know if you've ever been through one, but they're not easy, man. Really difficult.

**I hear plenty of amens from our readers.**

We were about to buy more than ten acres of land in Orange County right off the freeway. It was a beautiful piece of land—and it was going to cost $20 million just for the land, and then over $30 million for the different phases.

And I was thinking, *Why am I doing this?*

To be frank, I started asking myself, "How many of these church people will really *do* anything? Maybe 20 percent like most churches. Am I just building a bigger shoebox for people to sit and listen and leave? Do I want to raise all this money for a bigger shoebox?"

I was going through my "reluctant pastor" phase. It was probably part of my midlife reorientation, but I was really questioning what I was doing and whether it was worth it. Were there more mantras like this that I had applied that weren't really what I believed?

In the midst of this, I went to Bangkok with some strong CEO-type business leaders.

**What happened in Bangkok?**

We met with a missionary who spoke to us about his work, and he really emphasized his despair over Bangkok: "We've been here for more than a hundred years, and just one percent of the population is Christian." He described the sex industry, the mafia, and so forth, a dark and negative portrayal. But much of what he said was true.

As he was speaking, I noticed something I hadn't felt in a while: surges of excitement. *Why am I feeling so much energy right now?* I wondered. I was in the midst of something so much bigger than me, something so beyond human capacity. Things I couldn't figure out. A huge city with complex problems—and I realized that's what had been missing.

Things had gotten too predictable at my church. I was just running a big congregation.

In the end I felt God was saying I needed to move to Bangkok—right away.

"But God," I argued, "the church is growing. We're right in the middle of a lot of things, including a capital campaign. C'mon, not now!"

*No*, he seemed to say, *you've got to go now.*

So I went home, told the story to the leaders. Amazingly, they were overwhelmingly affirming. Some were crying, but they said, "You've got to go." So we changed the fundraising campaign. We raised money not just for buildings, but for furthering the cause of Christ all around the world and especially Thailand—and they sent me off with my family. My children agreed to go, which was a shock, by the way.

**How long were you intending to be there?**

At least one year. It was a great change of pace. In Bangkok, you don't drive, you walk. There's a lot of time for reflection while walking from place to place. I had time to sleep real well and time to think. I visited other churches and discovered that the Evangelical Covenant denomination there had 4,000 people in roughly [200] churches. It hit me. Back home NewSong had about 4,000 in four congregations.

I saw four churches with 4,000 people versus [200] churches with the same number of people, and the question I felt God posing to me is, *Who's stronger?*

**So who is stronger?**

The [two] hundred churches. You could knock any one of them out, and the rest would keep going. So much of our default protocol is centralized and built around one leader.

That same year I visited Vietnam. Have you heard of the Cu Chi Tunnels? They were dug underneath the fields—miles and miles of tunnels, dug with their hands. And they survived the onslaught of the biggest military force in the world. Actually, when the United States dropped napalm on that ground, it actually hardened and fortified those tunnels.

These guys were all about small units. And they were so resourceful. They would actually use the Americans' tools. When American planes would crash, they used the rubber from the tires as shoes. They could almost float in the water in the rice paddies. Whereas American soldiers would drop in with their boots and their 80-pound backpacks, and they were sitting ducks. I felt horrible for the Americans, out of their element. But looking at it from a Vietnamese perspective, the resourcefulness was tremendous.

**So a lot of times you don't want to go in big. You want to go in small.**

I started to ask what this meant for the church and our emphasis on bigger and bigger. We decided to launch organic-sized churches. Not house churches, but mid-sized.

**By mid-sized, you mean ...**

From 30 to 300. Most verges will probably be 30 to 100. That size has a lot of power especially for young adults, because they want intimacy but they also want the energy of a larger group.

Something as small as a house church is very fragile, not sustainable in many cases. And if you look at how modern armies and special forces move, they work in units of three, 12 through 30, and about 300. My guess is the biggest movement in churches of the future will be among those 30 to 300.

We call them *verges*, short for *convergence*, because they are a convergence of the best features of a small and a large church. I believe this size is going to be the most effective in many places around the world.

At the same time I was learning the absolute necessity of letting local people lead in this kind of church planting. You have to believe that the locals know more than you.

This is not always easy for an outsider from a powerful corporation or nation or church to believe. But innovation always happens on the fringe, and the larger an organization is, the more removed the leaders are from the growing edges where real change can take place.

You constantly have to fuel the fringe.

**So leaders of larger organizations can become isolated at the center?**

Absolutely, because you get larger, you give more attention to internal systems to keep the machine going. So you're not in touch many times with the little movements on the fringes. Yet the next significant thing will probably start as little movements on the fringe.

I also learned I needed to lift up local leadership—we don't always come with that mindset. We had to learn it. We have to believe that the locals really do know more than we do!

**We're sort of trained to assume David needs Saul's armor—that leaders need a certain structure.**

Yes, Saul really wanted him to use the armor, but David tried it on and said, "No, that's not going to work for me." He preferred his slingshot.

I began to realize that as a young church planter, working the church growth principles like crazy, I had been wearing someone else's armor. I began to realize maybe it didn't fit that well. Then I was reading about Gideon in Judges 7, where God whittled down his army from 32,000 to 300 men.

**There's that 300 again.**

It seemed like the Lord was saying, *Dave, what do you want? Do you want 30,000, or do you want 300 radicals?* I remember boldly saying, "Three hundred, Lord! Yeah, three hundred warriors!"

So I was fired up. But after that year in Bangkok, I came back to California and assumed my church understood the vision and values. I started asking, "Are we willing to give up our buildings? Are we willing to decentralize into many forms, many different sizes? To focus more on third culture leadership than on Sunday morning experiences? Are we willing to move into Santa Ana, not far from Irvine but with an under-resourced population we've neglected so far?"

**Wow. How'd that message go over?**

I started sharing that vision, and people started leaving. We had a 25-percent reduction in people and in giving over a year. I remember thinking, *God, I didn't really mean it.*

Many were disappointed in me. I think they just wanted to celebrate having me back, to have a time where instead of talking about mission and change, they could just say, "We just missed you, Dave." But I thought they were ready to hear the Word in a new way.

From the beginning of NewSong, we had a dream of planting a church in every major urban center in the world. But the form we were trying to replicate was the megachurch model. Of course, to have a megachurch, you have to have a megaleader.

So I was always looking for the capital-L Leader, the Bill Hybels-type leader. And the truth is, that kind of person is very hard to find.

**Oh, c'mon, there must be at least six of them, worldwide. *(Laughter.)***

Yes. And in the meantime I'd been ignoring some really great people. To be honest, I wouldn't pay as much attention to them. I began to realize I had missed a lot of opportunity to develop leaders who could lead really well with groups of 30 to 300.

Then we did a cost analysis. How much did we spend each month for this building? I think it was about $70,000 a month. And how much space did we use? About 30 percent of the space in a given month.

Well, in an urban center, every square foot is big dollars. Add parking lots, and you're talking major money going down the chute. For what? I realized I wasn't being a good steward of space. You certainly can't reproduce the megachurch model around the world in most urban settings. How are you going to do that in London or Mexico City? There churches will have to be creative in use of space and development of indigenous leaders.

**What did you learn about leadership from your time in Bangkok?**

At first, we were ramping it up according to the megachurch model. People were wowed. We had several hundred coming out, and not many had seen that before in Thailand. Then one of our leaders, a young man named Mehta, came up after one of our services looking very disappointed.

"Dave, this isn't NewSong," he said.

"What do you mean?" I asked, but inside I'm thinking, *Hey, man, I started NewSong!*

But he said, "We say we're about everybody getting involved, but only one person is speaking, only a few are leading worship, few people are doing anything. The rest are just sitting there. Before, when we met in our smaller groups, our verges, we were in circles. Now we're in rows."

I took a step back. I realized he knew this culture better than I did. "Okay, Mehta. What do you think we should do?"

**What did he think should happen?**

Smaller units. Decentralized. We ended up creating smaller units all over the city. People don't like to drive in Bangkok—it's too difficult to get across the city. So we created what we call undergrounds. They can meet in cafes, restaurants, academic buildings. They meet everywhere.

And to tell you the truth, if we had gone the megachurch direction, it would have required huge resources. Instead, now after two years, they're self-sustaining, meeting in cafes, clubs, restaurants, and homes.

**When you do church this way, it means handing off leadership into smaller groups. Do you worry about a loss of control and uneven quality?**

No. This is how real movements of God start. Bigness can slow you down. There's nothing wrong with bigness, by the way. I've seen beautiful whales in the ocean, man. I've seen them dance and splash in the water. Those are miraculous moments. They're magnificent creatures. But the truth is there aren't a lot of whales. But there are millions maybe billions of minnows. I like both big and small. But assuming big is better can hurt us, especially if we consider cultures, cities, and God's focus on the weak and the fringe of culture.

I don't think bigness is going to fit most people or most cultural contexts where the church needs to grow.

**Does this imply a new level of trust in God, rather than in systems that can scale predictably?**

I meet a lot of pastors, and many of them see pastoring like a job—they're just tending the machinery nine-to-five. I think the next movement has to shift toward saying, "I'm willing to sacrifice my pastoral job and be bi-vocational ... do whatever it takes."

The truth is that it's harder to make a living with a mid-sized, organic model. So if you really believe in this, embrace the fact that you're going to have to support yourself with another job. I've started doing that myself. I'm a partner in several outside ventures—a commodity trading firm, a non-profit called Xealot, a Web startup called [Yangdang.com]. I don't have to be a pastor to support my family. In fact, I'm a better pastor because I have other occupations. My jobs change; my calling remains the same.

**We've been asking, "Is our gospel too small?" It sounds like you've been rethinking what counts as big and small.**

I love the church. It's God's vehicle for transformation. But I don't want the church to become so centralized that it can't reproduce, can't quickly adopt multiple forms. And that works better when you're small, when you're on the verge, on the edge. Small is the new big. Big isn't bad, but it's overrated.

If the core of the gospel means truly loving God and our neighbor, then individual churches may not get big. But the church will be more enduring and virile than ever.

When the world, especially the up and coming generations, sees the church willing to forego size and instead loving people who are not like us, treating them as neighbors, it's a thing of beauty. And it's irresistible.

# Notes

1. Thomas L. Friedman, *The World Is Flat* (New York: Farrar, Straus, and Giroux, 2005).
2. David Brooks, "Harmony and the Dream," *New York Times* (August 11, 2008).
3. T. Masuda and R. E. Nisbett, "Attending Holistically vs. Analytically: Comparing the Context Sensitivity of Japanese and Americans," *Journal of Personality and Social Psychology* 81 (2001): 922–34.
4. Judith M. Gundry Volf and Miroslav Volf, *A Spacious Heart: Essays on Identity and Belonging* (Leominster, UK: Gracewing, 1997), 58–59.
5. Ibid.
6. See Lausanne Committee for World Evangelization, "Lausanne Occasional Paper 1: Pasadena Consultation—Homogeneous Unit Principle" (paper produced by the consultation, held May 31 to June 2, 1977, in Pasadena, California), 1978; http://www.lausanne.org/pasadena-1977/lop-1.html.
7. Ibid.

8. http://youtube.com/watch?v=1orA2iCkEpI&feature=related.
9. By the way, when I refer to new models, the truth is that they may be new to us but not really new historically or to others. The new forms may actually be old forms but with variations on style, ethos, language, or design.
10. Rodney Stark, *The Rise of Christianity: How the Obscure, Marginal, Jesus Movement Became the Dominant Religious Force in the Western World in a Few Centuries* (San Francisco: HarperSanFrancisco, 1997), 82.
11. Thomas L. Friedman, *The Lexus and the Olive Tree* (New York: Anchor, 2000), 15.
12. Frans Johansson, *The Medici Effect* (Boston: Harvard Business School Press, 2006), 79.

# About the Leadership Network Innovation Series

Since 1984, Leadership Network has fostered church innovation and growth by diligently pursuing its far-reaching mission statement: *To identify high-capacity Christian leaders, to connect them with other leaders, and to help them multiply their impact.*

While specific techniques may vary as the church faces new opportunities and challenges, Leadership Network consistently focuses on bringing together entrepreneurial leaders who are pursuing similar ministry initiatives. The resulting peer-to-peer interaction, dialogue, and collaboration—often across denominational lines—helps these leaders better refine their individual strategies and accelerate their own innovations.

To further enhance this process, Leadership Network develops and distributes highly targeted ministry tools and resources, including books, DVDs and videotapes, special reports, e-publications, and free downloads.

Launched in 2006, the Leadership Network Innovation Series presents case studies and insights from leading practitioners and pioneering churches that are successfully navigating the ever-changing streams of spiritual renewal in modern society. Each book offers *real* stories, about *real* leaders, in *real* churches, doing *real* ministry. Readers gain honest and thorough analyses, transferable principles, and clear guidance on how to put proven ideas to work in their individual settings.

With the assistance of Leadership Network—and the Leadership Network Innovation Series—today's Christian leaders are energized, equipped, inspired, and enabled to multiply their own dynamic kingdom-building initiatives. And the pace of innovative ministry is growing as never before.

For additional information on the mission or activities of Leadership Network, please contact:

LEADERSHIP NETWORK®

800-765-5323
www.leadnet.org
client.care@leadnet.org

*The Leadership Network Innovation Series*

# Leadership from the Inside Out

## Examining the Inner Life of a Healthy Church Leader

*Kevin Harney*

You can serve God and his people for a lifetime and do it with passion and joy. You do not have to become one of the growing number of leaders who have compromised their integrity, character, and ministry because they failed to lead an examined and accountable life.

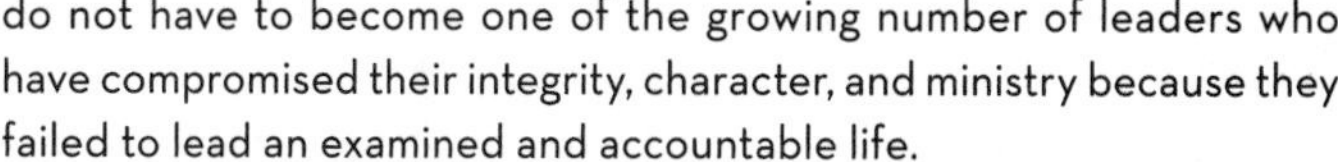

The road forward is clearly marked. Leaders must decide to humbly and consistently examine their inner lives and identify areas of needed change and growth. Also, wise leaders commit to listen to the voices of those who will love them enough to speak the truth and point out problems and potential pitfalls.

Kevin Harney writes, "The vision of this book is to assist leaders as they discover the health, wisdom, and joy of living an examined life. It is also to give practical tools for self-examination." Sharing stories and wisdom from his years in ministry, Harney shows you how to maintain the most powerful tool in your leadership toolbox: you. Your heart, so you can love well. Your mind, so you can continue to learn and grow. Your ears, your eyes, your mouth.... Consider this your essential guide to conducting a complete interior health exam, so you can spot and fix any problems, preserve the things that matter most, and grow as a source of vision, strength, and hope to others.

Softcover: 978-0-310-25943-5

## The Leadership Network Innovation Series

# Sticky Church

*Larry Osborne*

In *Sticky Church*, author and pastor Larry Osborne makes the case that closing the back door of your church is even more important than opening the front door wider. He offers a time-tested strategy for doing so: sermon-based small groups that dig deeper into the weekend message and Velcro™ members to the ministry. It's a strategy that enabled Osborne's congregation to grow from a handful of people to one of the larger churches in the nation—without any marketing or special programming.

*Sticky Church* tells the inspiring story of North Coast Church's phenomenal growth and offers practical tips for launching your own sermon-based small group ministry. Topics include:

Why stickiness is so important
Why most of our discipleship models don't work very well
Why small groups always make a church more honest and transparent
What makes groups grow deeper and stickier over time

*Sticky Church* is an ideal book for church leaders who want to start or retool their small group ministry—and Velcro™ their congregation to the Bible and each other.

Softcover: 978-0-310-28508-3

# Deliberate Simplicity

## How the Church Does More by Doing Less

*David Browning*

Less is more. And more is better. This is the new equation for church development, an equation with eternal results.

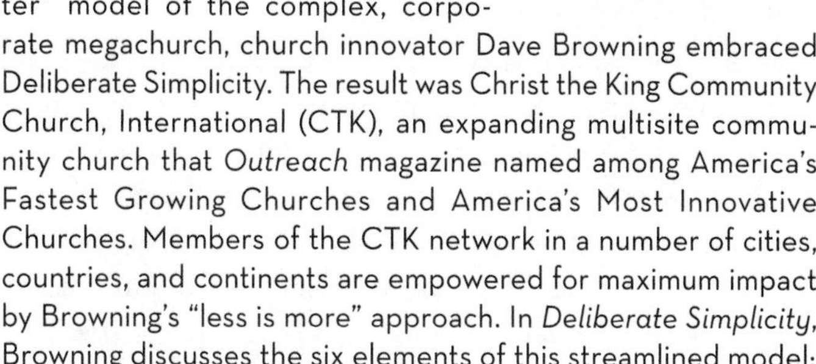

Rejecting the "bigger is better" model of the complex, corporate megachurch, church innovator Dave Browning embraced Deliberate Simplicity. The result was Christ the King Community Church, International (CTK), an expanding multisite community church that *Outreach* magazine named among America's Fastest Growing Churches and America's Most Innovative Churches. Members of the CTK network in a number of cities, countries, and continents are empowered for maximum impact by Browning's "less is more" approach. In *Deliberate Simplicity*, Browning discusses the six elements of this streamlined model:

- Minimality: Keep it simple
- Intentionality: Keep it missional
- Reality: Keep it real
- Multility: Keep it cellular
- Velocity: Keep it moving
- Scalability: Keep it expanding

As part of the Leadership Network Innovation Series, *Deliberate Simplicity* is a guide for church leaders seeking new strategies for more effective ministry.

Softcover: 978-0-310-28567-0

## Starting a Church Revolution through Serving

*Author: Dino Rizzo*

The world is wealthier than ever, yet poverty persists. Despite huge advancements in medicine, there are still millions dying from curable or preventable diseases. And even though there are more Christian workers and missionaries than ever before, divorce, abuse, addictions, and pain are still a reality for millions. The world is hurting and in need of hope and healing. Next-generation believers have an increasing passion to change their world. This book encourages that passion by telling real-life stories of how to reach out to the poor and hurting, by illustrating how a collection of individuals who are surrendered to Christ can truly make a difference in the world, and by showing the need for a revolution in serving—servolution.

This book shares stories from Healing Place Church's own servolution, coupled with practical guidelines and tips, and relaying what God has taught along the way. Dino Rizzo shares the good, the bad, and the ugly—not just the celebrations but also the "uh-oh's" and the "oh no's."

Softcover: 978-0-310-28763-6